Mmmm...
Chicken

Mmmm...
Chicken

First published in 2011
LOVE FOOD is an imprint of Parragon Books Ltd

Parragon
Queen Street House
4 Queen Street
Bath BA1 1HE, UK

ISBN: 978-1-4454-2439-2

Printed in China

Internal design by Talking Design
Introduction by Linda Doeser

Notes for the Reader
This book uses both metric and imperial measurements. Follow the same units of
measurement throughout; do not mix metric and imperial. All spoon measurements are
level: teaspoons are assumed to be 5 ml, and tablespoons are assumed to be 15 ml.
Unless otherwise stated, milk is assumed to be full fat, eggs and individual vegetables are
medium, and pepper is freshly ground black pepper.

The times given are an approximate guide only. Preparation times differ according to the
techniques used by different people and the cooking times may also vary from those
given. Optional ingredients, variations or serving suggestions have not been included in
the calculations.

Recipes using raw or very lightly cooked eggs should be avoided by infants, the elderly,
pregnant women, convalescents and anyone suffering from an illness. Pregnant and
breastfeeding women are advised to avoid eating peanuts and peanut products.
Sufferers from nut allergies should be aware that some of the ready-made ingredients
used in the recipes in this book may contain nuts. Always check the packaging before use.

contents

introduction

Chicken is a popular favourite with adults and children alike, perhaps because it is such a versatile ingredient that there are heaps of different dishes to suit all tastes. It can be prepared in lots of ways, from classic roasts to speedy stir-fries and from spicy curries to rich and satisfying stews. It makes great sandwiches, wraps, salads, soups and kebabs and is the perfect partner for pasta and rice. It is perfect for any occasion from an elegant dinner party with friends to a relaxed family barbecue.

The delicate flavour of chicken combines well with many kinds of other ingredients and cooks in every corner of the world have created their own unique repertoire of chicken dishes. Ginger, soy sauce, noodles, lemon grass, chillies and fresh coriander feature in Asian dishes, while olives, wine, garlic, tomatoes and ham characterize Mediterranean recipes.

A subtle use of herbs and spices brings out the full flavour of chicken. Tarragon, with its slight hint of aniseed and basil, works particularly well, while piquant hot spices are typical of Mexican, Caribbean and Indian cuisines and warm aromatic spices feature in Middle Eastern and Cajun dishes. Common accompaniments to chicken include honey, sherry, prawns, fruit, especially citrus fruit, cheese, mushrooms and all kinds of vegetables.

Not only is chicken a versatile ingredient, it can also have health benefits. Chicken is an excellent source of protein, B vitamins and minerals, and is naturally low in fat, making it an ideal ingredient if you are watching your weight. It is important to remove the skin before cooking and eating chicken, as this is where the fat is. The B vitamins that chicken contain are important in our diet as they help release energy from our food into our body.

buying, storing & preparing chicken

• When choosing a fresh chicken look for one with a plump breast and creamy-coloured skin. The tip of the breast bone should be pliable. These days chicken is almost always sold oven-ready (that is, plucked and cleaned) although the giblets – heart, liver, neck and gizzard – may be included, particularly with frozen birds.

The smallest birds are four- to six-week-old poussins which weigh 450–550 g/1–1 lb 4 oz and make a perfect serving for one. Double poussins are eight to ten weeks old, weigh 800–900 g/1 lb 12 oz–2 lb and will serve two people. Three-month-old spring chickens, ideal for three to four people, weigh 1–1.25 kg/2 lb 4 oz–2 lb 12 oz, while roasters are twice this age and weigh 1.5–2 kg/3 lb 5 oz–4 lb 8 oz. Boiling fowl, which make superb soups and good stews as long as they are cooked gently for 2–3 hours, are usually about a year old and weigh 2–3 kg/ 4 lb 8 oz–6 lb 8 oz. Corn-fed chickens have an attractive yellow coloration and are about the same size as roasters. As they are usually free-range and often organically raised rather than intensively reared, they tend to be a little more expensive.

A wide variety of chicken pieces are available. It is often more economical to buy a whole bird and cut it into serving pieces yourself, but ready prepared pieces are very convenient. The leg consists of drumstick and thigh meat and is a good choice for casseroles and stews. Drumsticks are great for frying and a popular choice for barbecues. Thighs are also good for slow cooking methods and skinless boneless thighs are ideal for stuffing. Chicken breasts have a milder flavour than the dark meat and are good for stuffing, stir-frying or pan-frying in butter. While chicken wings don't have much meat, they make popular nibbles at barbecues or pan-fried as a starter. Diced and minced chicken pieces are also widely available, although it is easy to prepare these at home using skinless, boneless chicken breasts.

• Store frozen birds in the freezer and thaw completely before cooking. To do this, open one end of the bag and put the chicken in a cool place for up to 12 hours. Smaller birds, such as poussins, will take less time. Remove the giblets, if there are any, as soon as you can. The chicken is ready for cooking when the legs are soft and flexible and there are no ice crystals in the cavity. You can speed up the process slightly by putting the bird, without opening the bag, in a bowl of cold water. Do not try to thaw frozen chicken in hot water.

• Store fresh birds on a plate, loosely covered with greaseproof paper or clingfilm on the bottom shelf of the refrigerator. Cook within three days of purchase.

• Raw chicken may contain salmonella and other bacteria that can cause food poisoning so always wash the chopping board, knives and other utensils thoroughly after preparing it. Ideally, keep a specific chopping board for poultry that is dishwasher safe so it can withstand high temperatures. Wash your hands both before and after handling raw chicken and before touching any other ingredients. Do not rinse the chicken under cold running water. Although this may seem like a sensible precaution, it's more likely to spread bacteria not only over the chicken but also all over the kitchen than to get rid of them.

• When cooking on a barbecue, make sure that you do not use the forks, knives, tongs and so on for other ingredients after using them

for chicken, unless they have been thoroughly washed in hot soapy water first.

• Thorough cooking destroys the bacteria and it is very important that chicken is cooked all the way through before serving. Test by inserting the point of a sharp knife in the thickest part of the meat. If the juices run clear, it is ready. If there are any traces of pink, cook for a few minutes more and test again. Check too that the base of the cut is firm and white. The thickest part on a whole bird is the inside of the thigh.

• If you're planning to stuff a chicken for roasting, do so just before putting it into the oven. Pack the stuffing loosely and remember to weigh the chicken afterwards to calculate the cooking time. Leftover stuffing may be cooked separately. Don't stuff the body cavity of a large bird as it may not cook all the way through. Allow 20 minutes per 450 g/1 lb, plus 20 minutes extra at 200°C/400°F/Gas Mark 6 in a preheated oven. When the chicken is cooked through, remove it from the oven, cover with foil and leave to rest for 10–15 minutes before carving.

chicken stock

makes about 2.5 litres/4½ pints

- 1.3 kg/3 lb chicken wings and necks
- 2 onions, cut into wedges
- 4 litres/7 pints water
- 2 carrots, roughly chopped
- 2 celery sticks, roughly chopped
- 10 fresh parsley sprigs
- 4 fresh thyme sprigs
- 2 bay leaves
- 10 black peppercorns

1 Place the chicken wings and necks and the onions in a large saucepan and cook over a low heat, stirring frequently, until lightly browned.

2 Add the water and stir well to scrape off any sediment from the base of the pan. Gradually bring to the boil, skimming off the foam that rises to the surface. Add all the remaining ingredients, partially cover and simmer for 3 hours.

3 Strain the stock into a bowl, leave to cool, cover and store in the refrigerator. When cold, discard the layer of fat from the surface. Use immediately or freeze for up to 6 months.

mole sauce

serves 6–10

- 9 mixed chillies, soaked in hot water for 30 minutes and drained
- 1 onion, sliced
- 2–3 garlic cloves, crushed
- 85 g/3 oz sesame seeds
- 85 g/3 oz toasted flaked almonds
- 1 tsp ground coriander
- 4 cloves
- ½ tsp pepper
- 2–3 tbsp sunflower oil
- 300 ml/10 fl oz chicken or vegetable stock
- 450 g/1 lb ripe tomatoes, peeled and chopped
- 2 tsp ground cinnamon
- 55 g/2 oz raisins
- 140 g/5 oz pumpkin seeds
- 55 g/2 oz plain chocolate, broken into pieces
- 1 tbsp red wine vinegar

1 Put the chillies in a food processor with the onion, garlic, sesame seeds, almonds, coriander, cloves and pepper and process to form a thick paste.

2 Heat the oil in a saucepan, add the paste, and fry for 5 minutes. Add the stock with the tomatoes, cinnamon, raisins and pumpkin seeds.

3 Bring to the boil, reduce the heat and simmer, stirring occasionally, for 15 minutes.

4 Add the chocolate and vinegar to the sauce. Cook gently for 5 minutes, then use as required.

Mmmm...
starters, soups & salads

chicken pâté

serves 4
- 140 g/5 oz butter
- 1 onion, finely chopped
- 1 garlic clove, finely chopped
- 250 g/9 oz chicken livers
- ½ tsp Dijon mustard
- 2 tbsp brandy (optional)
- brown toast fingers, to serve
- salt and pepper

clarified butter (optional)
- 115 g/4 oz lightly salted butter

1 Melt half the butter in a large frying pan over a medium heat and cook the onion for 3–4 minutes until soft and transparent. Add the garlic and continue to cook for a further 2 minutes.

2 Check the chicken livers and remove any discoloured parts using a pair of scissors. Add the livers to the frying pan and cook over quite a high heat for 5–6 minutes until they are brown in colour.

3 Season well with salt and pepper and add the mustard and brandy, if using.

4 Process the pâté in a blender or food processor until smooth. Add the remaining butter cut into small pieces and process again until creamy.

5 Press the pâté into a serving dish or 4 small ramekins, smooth over the surface and cover with clingfilm. If the pâté is to be kept for more than 2 days, you could cover the surface with a little clarified butter. In a clean saucepan, heat the butter until it melts, then continue heating for a few moments until it stops bubbling. Allow the sediment to settle and carefully pour the clarified butter over the pâté.

6 Chill in the refrigerator until ready to serve, accompanied by toast fingers.

chicken balls with dipping sauce

serves 4

- 3 tbsp vegetable oil
- 2 large skinless, boneless chicken breasts, cut into 2-cm/¾-inch pieces
- 2 shallots, finely chopped
- ½ celery stick, finely chopped
- 1 garlic clove, crushed
- 2 tbsp light soy sauce
- 1 small egg
- 1 bunch of spring onions, trimmed, to serve
- salt and pepper

dipping sauce

- 3 tbsp dark soy sauce
- 1 tbsp rice wine
- 1 tsp sesame seeds

1 Heat half of the oil in a frying pan and stir-fry the chicken over a high heat for 2–3 minutes until golden. Remove from the pan and set aside. Add the shallots, celery and garlic to the pan pan and and stir-fry for 1–2 minutes until softened.

2 Place the chicken, shallots, celery and garlic in a food processor and process until finely minced. Add 1 tablespoon of the light soy sauce and just enough egg to make a fairly firm mixture. Season to taste with salt and pepper.

3 Make the dipping sauce by mixing together the dark soy sauce, rice wine and sesame seeds in a small serving bowl and set aside.

4 Shape the chicken mixture into 16–18 walnut-sized balls. Heat the remaining oil in the frying pan or wok and stir-fry the chicken balls in small batches for 4–5 minutes until golden brown. As each batch is cooked drain on kitchen paper and keep hot.

5 Add the spring onions to the pan or wok and stir-fry for 1–2 minutes until they begin to soften, then stir in the remaining light soy sauce. Serve the chicken balls with the stir-fried spring onions and the bowl of dipping sauce.

chicken satay skewers with peanut sauce

serves 4

- 4 skinless, boneless chicken breasts, about 115 g/4 oz each, cut into 2-cm/¾-inch cubes
- 4 tbsp soy sauce
- 1 tbsp cornflour
- 2 garlic cloves, finely chopped
- 2.5-cm/1-inch piece fresh ginger, peeled and finely chopped
- cucumber, roughly chopped, to serve

peanut sauce

- 2 tbsp groundnut or vegetable oil
- ½ onion, finely chopped
- 1 garlic clove, finely chopped
- 4 tbsp crunchy peanut butter
- 4–5 tbsp water
- ½ tsp chilli powder

1 Put the chicken cubes in a shallow dish. Mix the soy sauce, cornflour, garlic and ginger together in a small bowl and pour over the chicken. Cover and leave to marinate in the refrigerator for at least 2 hours.

2 Meanwhile, soak 12 bamboo skewers in cold water for at least 30 minutes. Preheat the grill, thread the chicken pieces onto the bamboo skewers. Transfer the skewers to a griddle pan and cook under a preheated grill for 3–4 minutes. Turn the skewers over and cook for a further 3–4 minutes or until cooked through.

3 Meanwhile, to make the sauce, heat the oil in the saucepan, add the onion and garlic and cook over a medium heat, stirring frequently, for 3–4 minutes until softened. Add the peanut butter, water and chilli powder and simmer for 2–3 minutes until softened and thinned. Serve the skewers immediately with the warm sauce and cucumber.

sticky ginger & soy chicken wings

serves 4

- 12 chicken wings
- 2 garlic cloves, crushed
- 2.5-cm/1-inch piece fresh ginger
- 2 tbsp dark soy sauce
- 2 tbsp lime juice
- 1 tbsp clear honey
- 1 tsp chilli sauce
- 2 tsp sesame oil
- lime wedges, to serve

1 Tuck the pointed tip of each wing under the thicker end to make a neat triangle.

2 Mix together the garlic, ginger, soy sauce, lime, honey, chilli sauce and oil.

3 Spoon the mixture over the chicken and turn to coat evenly. Cover and marinate for several hours or overnight.

4 Preheat the grill to hot. Cook the wings on a foil-lined grill pan for 12–15 minutes, or until the juices have no trace of pink when pierced, basting often with the marinade. Serve hot with lime wedges.

buffalo wings

serves 12
- 5 tbsp dark soy sauce
- 2 tbsp dry sherry
- 1 tbsp rice vinegar
- juice of 1 orange and 5-cm/2-inch strip of orange rind, pith removed
- 1 tbsp muscovado sugar
- 1 star anise
- 1 tsp cornflour, mixed to a paste with 3 tbsp water
- 1 tbsp finely chopped fresh ginger
- 1 tsp chilli sauce
- 1.5 kg/3 lb 5 oz chicken wings

1 Preheat the oven to 200°C/400°F/Gas Mark 6. Place the soy sauce, sherry, vinegar, orange rind, sugar and star anise into a saucepan, add the juice extracted from the orange and mix well. Bring to the boil over a medium heat, then stir in the cornflour paste. Continue to boil, stirring constantly, for 1 minute, or until thickened.

2 Remove the saucepan from the heat and stir in the ginger and chilli sauce. Remove and discard the tips from the chicken wings and place the wings in a single layer in an ovenproof dish or roasting tin. Pour the sauce over the wings, turning and stirring to coat.

3 Bake in the oven for 35–40 minutes, turning and basting with the sauce occasionally, until the chicken is tender and browned and the juices run clear when a skewer is inserted into the thickest part of the meat. Serve either hot or warm.

grilled chicken wings with tahini sauce

serves 4–6
- 8 chicken wings, halved
- warmed pitta bread, to serve

marinade
- 3 tbsp olive oil
- 2 tsp smoked Spanish paprika
- 1 tsp cumin seeds, crushed
- ½ tsp dried oregano
- 2 large garlic cloves, crushed
- salt and pepper

tahini sauce
- 1 large garlic clove, crushed
- ¼ tsp salt
- 125 ml/4 fl oz tahini, well stirred
- juice of 1½ lemons
- 6–8 tbsp water

1 Put the chicken wings in a shallow dish. Combine the marinade ingredients and rub into the chicken. Cover and leave to marinate in the refrigerator for 2–24 hours. Allow to come to room temperature before cooking.

2 To make the sauce, crush the garlic and salt to a paste, using a mortar and pestle. Transfer to a blender with the tahini and lemon juice. Process until smooth, adding enough water to make a creamy sauce. Pour into a serving bowl and set aside.

3 Preheat the grill. Place the wings on a rack in a foil-lined grill pan, and brush with the oily marinade remaining in the dish. Position the pan about 15 cm/6 inches from the heat source and grill for 12–15 minutes, turning once, until golden and the juices run clear when pierced with a skewer. Tip into a serving bowl and pour over the pan juices.

4 Serve with the tahini sauce and fingers of pitta bread.

oven-fried chicken wings

serves 4

- 12 chicken wings
- 1 egg
- 50 ml/2 fl oz milk
- 4 heaped tbsp plain flour
- 1 tsp paprika
- salt and pepper
- 225 g/8 oz breadcrumbs
- 55 g/2 oz butter

1 Preheat the oven to 220°C/425°F/Gas Mark 7. Separate the chicken wings into 3 pieces each. Discard the bony tip. Beat the egg with the milk in a shallow dish. Combine the flour, paprika and salt and pepper to taste in a separate shallow dish. Place the breadcrumbs in another shallow dish.

2 Dip the chicken pieces into the egg to coat well, then drain and roll in the seasoned flour. Remove, shaking off any excess, and roll the chicken in the breadcrumbs, gently pressing them onto the surface, then shaking off any excess.

3 Melt the butter in the preheated oven in a shallow roasting tin large enough to hold all the chicken pieces in a single layer. Arrange the chicken, skin-side down, in the tin and bake in the oven for 10 minutes. Turn and bake for a further 10 minutes, or until the chicken is tender and the juices run clear when a skewer is inserted into the thickest part of the meat.

4 Remove the chicken from the tin and arrange on a large platter. Serve hot or at room temperature.

asian-style fried chicken

serves 4

- 6 skinless, boneless chicken thighs, about 100 g/3½ oz each
- 4 tbsp shoyu (Japanese soy sauce)
- 4 tbsp mirin
- 2 tsp finely grated fresh ginger
- 2 garlic cloves, crushed
- oil, for deep-frying
- 70 g/2½ oz potato flour or cornflour
- pinch of salt
- lemon wedges, to serve

1 Cut the chicken into large cubes and put in a bowl. Add the shoyu, mirin, ginger and garlic and turn the chicken to coat well. Cover with clingfilm and marinate in a cool place for 20 minutes.

2 Heat a large wok over a high heat. Pour in the oil and heat to 180°C/350°F or until a cube of bread browns in 30 seconds.

3 Meanwhile, mix the potato flour with the salt in a bowl. Lift the chicken out of the marinade and shake off any excess. Drop it into the potato flour and coat well, then shake off any excess.

4 Add the chicken to the oil, in batches, and cook for 6 minutes, or until crisp and brown. Remove, drain on kitchen paper and keep hot while you cook the remaining chicken.

5 Serve with lemon wedges.

chicken toasts

serves 4

- 12 slices French bread or rustic bread
- 4 tbsp olive oil
- 2 garlic cloves, chopped
- 2 tbsp finely chopped fresh oregano
- salt and pepper
- 100 g/3½ oz cold roast chicken, cut into small, thin slices
- 4 tomatoes, sliced
- 12 thin slices of goat's cheese
- 12 black olives, stoned and chopped
- fresh green salad leaves, to serve

1 Preheat the oven to 180°C/350°F/Gas Mark 4 and the grill to medium. Put the bread under the preheated grill and lightly toast on both sides. Meanwhile, pour the olive oil into a bowl and add the garlic and oregano. Season with salt and pepper and mix well. Remove the toasted bread slices from the grill and brush them on one side only with the oil mixture.

2 Place the bread slices, oiled sides up, on a baking sheet. Put some sliced chicken on top of each one, followed by a slice of tomato. Divide the slices of goat's cheese between them, then top with the chopped olives. Drizzle over the remaining oil mixture and transfer to the preheated oven. Bake for about 5 minutes, or until the cheese is golden and starting to melt. Remove from the oven and serve with fresh green salad leaves.

sherried chicken & bacon toasts

serves 2

- 2 tbsp olive oil
- 2 rindless bacon rashers, cut into strips
- 1 small onion, chopped
- 2 garlic cloves, chopped
- 1 bay leaf
- 2 fresh thyme sprigs
- 2 small skinless, boneless chicken breasts, cut into small chunks
- 1 tbsp wholegrain mustard
- 6 tbsp dry sherry
- 2 slices traditional white bread, 1.5 cm/¾ inch thick
- about 25 g/1 oz/1 tbsp butter, softened
- small handful of chopped parsley, stalks discarded
- 2 tbsp mild plain yogurt (optional)
- salt and pepper

1 Heat the oil in a frying pan and add the bacon, onion, garlic, bay leaf and thyme. Cook, stirring often, for 5 minutes, until the bacon and onion are cooked. Add the chicken and continue cooking for 5 minutes, stirring so that the chicken cooks evenly.

2 Add the mustard and sherry and bring to the boil, stirring all the sediment off the bottom of the pan. Add seasoning to taste. Simmer for 3–4 minutes, until the sherry is reduced to a mustard glaze on the ingredients. Discard the bay leaf and herb sprigs.

3 Meanwhile, preheat the grill to a medium–high setting and warm two plates. Place the bread on a rack in the grill pan and toast for about 2 minutes on each side, until evenly golden and crisp.

4 Butter the hot toast and place on the warmed plates. Stir the parsley into the chicken mixture and pile it on the toasts. Drizzle over a little yogurt, if liked, then serve immediately.

creamy chicken

serves 6
- 4 tbsp olive oil
- 900 g/2 lb skinless, boneless chicken, diced
- 125 g/4½ oz rindless smoked bacon, diced
- 12 shallots
- 2 garlic cloves, crushed
- 1 tbsp mild curry powder
- 300 ml/10 fl oz mayonnaise
- 1 tbsp clear honey
- 1 tbsp chopped fresh parsley
- pepper
- 85 g/3 oz seedless white grapes, quartered, to garnish
- cold saffron rice, to serve

1 Heat the oil in a large, heavy-based frying pan. Add the chicken, bacon, shallots, garlic and curry powder. Cook slowly, stirring, for about 15 minutes.

2 Spoon the mixture into a clean mixing bowl. Leave to cool completely, then season to taste with pepper.

3 Blend the mayonnaise with the honey, then add the parsley. Toss the chicken mixture in the mayonnaise mixture.

4 Place the chicken mixture in a serving dish, garnish with the grapes and serve with cold saffron rice.

chinese lemon chicken

serves 4
- 300 g/10½ oz skinless, boneless chicken breast
- chopped fresh herbs, to garnish

marinade
- 150 ml/5 fl oz freshly squeezed lemon juice
- 1 tbsp light soy sauce
- 1 tbsp cornflour

1 Cut the chicken into bite-sized cubes and place in a shallow dish.

2 Mix together the lemon juice and soy sauce in a bowl. Put the cornflour in another bowl and stir in the lemon and soy mixture to form a paste. Spread over the chicken and leave to marinate for 15 minutes.

3 Heat a non-stick frying pan and add the chicken and marinade. Cook, stirring, for 10–12 minutes, or until the chicken is thoroughly cooked. Transfer to 4 serving plates, pour over the sauce and serve, garnished with fresh herbs.

sautéed chicken with crispy garlic slices

serves 8

- 8 skin-on chicken thighs, boned if available
- hot or sweet smoked Spanish paprika, to taste
- 4 tbsp Spanish olive oil
- 10 garlic cloves, sliced
- 125 ml/4 fl oz dry white wine
- 1 bay leaf
- salt
- fresh parsley, chopped, to garnish
- crusty bread, to serve (optional)

1 If necessary, halve the chicken thighs and remove the bones, then cut the flesh into bite-sized pieces, leaving the skin on. Season with paprika.

2 Heat the oil in a large frying pan or a flameproof casserole, add the garlic slices and cook over a medium heat, stirring frequently, for 1 minute until golden brown. Remove with a slotted spoon and drain on kitchen paper.

3 Add the chicken thighs to the pan and cook, turning occasionally, for 10 minutes, or until tender and golden brown on all sides. Add the wine and bay leaf and bring to the boil. Reduce the heat and simmer, stirring occasionally, for 10 minutes, or until most of the liquid has evaporated and the juices run clear when a skewer is inserted into the thickest part of the meat. Season to taste with salt.

4 Transfer the chicken to a warmed serving dish and sprinkle over the reserved garlic slices. Scatter with chopped parsley to garnish and serve with chunks of crusty bread to mop up the juices, if desired.

chicken in lemon & garlic

serves 6-8

- 4 large skinless, boneless chicken breasts
- 5 tbsp extra virgin olive oil
- 1 onion, finely chopped
- 6 garlic cloves, finely chopped
- grated rind of 1 lemon, finely pared rind of 1 lemon and juice of both lemons
- 4 tbsp chopped fresh flat-leaf parsley
- salt and pepper
- lemon wedges and crusty bread, to serve

1 Using a sharp knife, slice the chicken breasts widthways into very thin slices. Heat the olive oil in a large, heavy-based frying pan, add the onion and fry for 5 minutes, or until softened but not browned. Add the garlic and fry for a further 30 seconds.

2 Add the sliced chicken to the pan and fry gently for 5–10 minutes, stirring from time to time, until all the ingredients are lightly browned and the chicken is tender.

3 Add the grated lemon rind and the lemon juice and let it bubble. At the same time, deglaze the pan by scraping and stirring all the bits on the base of the pan into the juices with a wooden spoon. Remove the pan from the heat, stir in the parsley and season to taste with salt and pepper.

4 Transfer the chicken in lemon and garlic to a warmed serving dish. Sprinkle with the pared lemon rind and serve, piping hot, with lemon wedges for squeezing over the chicken, accompanied by chunks or slices of crusty bread for mopping up the lemon and garlic juices.

chicken rolls with olives

serves 6–8

- 115 g/4 oz black Spanish olives in oil, drained and 2 tbsp oil reserved
- 140 g/5 oz butter, softened
- 4 tbsp fresh parsley, chopped
- 4 skinless, boneless chicken breasts

1 Preheat the oven to 200°C/400°F/Gas Mark 6. Stone and finely chop the olives. Mix together the olives, butter and parsley in a bowl.

2 Place the chicken breasts between 2 sheets of clingfilm and beat gently with a meat mallet or the side of a rolling pin.

3 Spread the olive and herb butter over one side of each flattened chicken breast and roll up. Secure with a wooden cocktail stick or tie with clean string if necessary.

4 Place the chicken rolls in an ovenproof dish. Drizzle over the oil from the olive jar and bake in the preheated oven for 45–55 minutes, or until tender and the juices run clear when the chicken is pierced with the point of a sharp knife.

5 Transfer the chicken rolls to a chopping board and discard the cocktail sticks or string. Using a sharp knife, cut into slices, then transfer to warmed serving plates and serve.

chicken & corn soup

serves 6

- 1 roasted chicken, about 1.3 kg/3 lb
- ½ tsp saffron threads
- 3 tbsp corn oil
- 2 onions, thinly sliced
- 3 celery sticks, sliced
- 1.7 litres/3 pints basic vegetable stock
- 8 black peppercorns
- 1 blade mace
- 115 g/4 oz egg noodles
- 400 g/14 oz frozen sweetcorn
- pinch of dried sage
- 2 tbsp chopped fresh parsley
- salt and pepper

1 Remove the skin from the chicken, cut the meat off the bones and cut into small pieces. Put the saffron into a bowl, pour in hot water to cover and leave to soak.

2 Heat the oil in a saucepan. Add the onions and celery and cook over a low heat, stirring occasionally, for 5 minutes, until softened. Increase the heat to medium, pour in the stock, add the peppercorns and mace and bring to the boil. Reduce the heat and simmer for 25 minutes.

3 Increase the heat to medium, add the chicken, noodles, sweetcorn, sage, parsley and saffron with its soaking water, season to taste with salt and pepper and bring back to the boil. Reduce the heat and simmer for a further 20 minutes.

4 Remove the pan from the heat, taste and adjust the seasoning, if necessary. Ladle into warmed bowls and serve immediately.

chicken & leek soup

serves 6–8

- 2 tbsp olive oil
- 2 onions, roughly chopped
- 2 carrots, roughly chopped
- 5 leeks, 2 roughly chopped, 3 thinly sliced
- 1 chicken, weighing 1.3 kg/3 lb
- 2 bay leaves
- 6 prunes, sliced
- salt and pepper
- sprigs of fresh parsley, to garnish

1 Heat the oil in a large saucepan over a medium heat, then add the onions, carrots and the 2 roughly chopped leeks. Sauté for 3–4 minutes until just golden brown. Wipe the chicken inside and out and remove any excess skin and fat.

2 Place the chicken in the saucepan with the cooked vegetables and add the bay leaves. Pour in enough cold water to just cover and season well with salt and pepper. Bring to the boil, reduce the heat, then cover and simmer for 1–1½ hours. From time to time skim off any scum that forms.

3 Remove the chicken from the stock, remove and discard the skin, then remove all the meat. Cut the meat into neat pieces.

4 Strain the stock through a colander, discard the vegetables and bay leaves and return to the rinsed-out saucepan. Expect to have 1.2–1.4 litres/2–2½ pints of stock. Blot the fat off the surface with pieces of kitchen paper.

5 Heat the stock to simmering point, add the sliced leeks and prunes to the saucepan and heat for about 1 minute.

6 Return the chicken to the pan and heat through. Serve immediately in warmed deep dishes. Garnish with the parsley.

cream of chicken soup

serves 4

- 3 tbsp butter
- 4 shallots, chopped
- 1 leek, sliced
- 450 g/1 lb skinless, boneless chicken breasts, chopped
- 600 ml/1 pint chicken stock
- 1 tbsp chopped fresh parsley
- 1 tbsp chopped fresh thyme, plus extra sprigs to garnish
- 175 ml/6 fl oz double cream
- salt and pepper

1 Melt the butter in a large saucepan over a medium heat. Add the shallots and cook, stirring, for 3 minutes, until slightly softened. Add the leek and cook for a further 5 minutes, stirring. Add the chicken, stock and herbs, and season to taste with salt and pepper. Bring to the boil, then lower the heat and simmer for 25 minutes, until the chicken is tender and cooked through. Remove from the heat and leave to cool for 10 minutes.

2 Transfer the soup to a food processor or blender and process until smooth (you may need to do this in batches). Return the soup to the rinsed-out pan and warm over a low heat for 5 minutes.

3 Stir in the cream and cook for a further 2 minutes, then remove from the heat and ladle into serving bowls. Garnish with sprigs of thyme and serve immediately.

chicken-noodle soup

serves 6–8

- 2 skinless chicken breasts
- 2 litres/3½ pints water
- 1 onion, unpeeled, halved
- 1 large garlic clove, halved
- 1-cm/½-inch piece fresh ginger, peeled and sliced
- 4 black peppercorns, lightly crushed
- 4 cloves
- 2 star anise
- 1 carrot, peeled
- 1 celery stick, chopped
- 100 g/3½ oz baby sweetcorn, halved lengthways
- 2 spring onions, finely shredded
- 115 g/4 oz dried rice vermicelli noodles
- salt and pepper

1 Put the chicken breasts and water in a saucepan over a high heat and bring to the boil. Lower the heat to its lowest setting and simmer, skimming the surface until no more foam rises. Add the onion, garlic, ginger, peppercorns, cloves, star anise and a pinch of salt, and continue to simmer for 20 minutes, or until the chicken is tender and cooked through.

2 Strain the chicken, reserving about 1.2 litres/2 pints of stock, but discarding any flavouring solids. (At this point you can leave the stock to cool and refrigerate overnight, so any fat solidifies and can be lifted off and discarded.) Meanwhile, grate the carrot along its length on the coarse side of a grater so you get long, thin strips. Return the stock to the rinsed-out saucepan with the carrot, celery, baby sweetcorn and spring onions and bring to the boil. Boil until the baby sweetcorn are almost tender, then add the noodles and continue boiling for 2 minutes.

3 Meanwhile, chop the chicken, add to the pan and continue cooking for about 1 minute longer until the chicken is reheated and the noodles are soft. Add seasoning to taste.

chicken & potato soup with bacon

serves 4
- 1 tbsp butter
- 2 garlic cloves, chopped
- 1 onion, sliced
- 250 g/9 oz smoked lean back bacon, chopped
- 2 large leeks, sliced
- 2 tbsp plain flour
- 1 litre/1¾ pints chicken stock
- 800 g/1 lb 12 oz potatoes, chopped
- 200 g/7 oz skinless, boneless chicken breast, chopped
- 4 tbsp double cream
- salt and pepper
- grilled bacon, to garnish

1 Melt the butter in a large saucepan over a medium heat. Add the garlic and onion and cook, stirring, for 3 minutes, until slightly softened. Add the chopped bacon and leeks and cook for a further 3 minutes, stirring.

2 In a bowl, mix the flour with enough stock to make a smooth paste, then stir it into the pan. Cook, stirring, for 2 minutes. Pour in the remaining stock, then add the potatoes and chicken. Season to taste with salt and pepper. Bring to the boil, then lower the heat and simmer for 25 minutes, until the chicken and potatoes are tender and cooked through.

3 Stir in the cream and cook for a further 2 minutes, then remove from the heat and ladle into serving bowls. Garnish with grilled bacon and serve immediately.

chicken, prawn & ham soup

serves 6

- 175 g/6 oz skinless, boneless chicken breast, very thinly sliced into strips
- 175 g/6 oz peeled raw prawns, halved if large
- 1 tsp cornflour
- 2 tsp water
- 1 small egg white, lightly beaten
- pinch of salt
- 1 litre/1¾ pints basic vegetable stock
- 175 g/6 oz honey-roast ham, very thinly sliced into strips
- salt and pepper
- chopped spring onions or snipped fresh chives, to garnish

1 Mix together the chicken and prawns in a bowl. Mix the cornflour to a paste with the water in another bowl and add to the mixture, together with the egg white and the salt, stirring well to coat.

2 Bring the stock to the boil in a saucepan over a medium heat. Add the chicken mixture and the ham and bring back to the boil. Reduce the heat and simmer for 1 minute. Taste and adjust the seasoning, if necessary, and remove from the heat. Ladle into warmed bowls, garnish with spring onions and serve immediately.

wonton soup

serves 6

- 175 g/6 oz minced chicken
- 55 g/2 oz peeled prawns, minced
- 1 spring onion, finely chopped
- 1 tsp finely chopped fresh ginger
- 1 tsp sugar
- 1 tbsp Chinese rice wine or dry sherry
- 2 tbsp light soy sauce
- 24 ready-made wonton wrappers
- 850 ml/1½ pints basic vegetable stock
- snipped fresh chives, to garnish

1 Mix together the chicken, prawns, spring onion, ginger, sugar, rice wine and half the soy sauce in a bowl until thoroughly combined. Cover and leave to marinate for 20 minutes.

2 Put 1 teaspoon of the mixture in the centre of each wonton wrapper. Dampen the edges, fold corner to corner into a triangle and press to seal, then seal the bottom corners together.

3 Bring the stock to the boil in a large saucepan. Add the wontons and cook for 5 minutes. Stir in the remaining soy sauce and remove from the heat. Ladle the soup and wontons into warmed bowls, sprinkle with snipped chives and serve immediately.

smoked chicken & cranberry salad

serves 4

- 1 smoked chicken, weighing 1.3 kg/3 lb
- 115 g/4 oz dried cranberries
- 2 tbsp apple juice or water
- 200 g/7 oz sugar snap peas
- 2 ripe avocados
- juice of ½ lemon
- 4 lettuce hearts
- 1 bunch of watercress, trimmed
- 55 g/2 oz rocket
- 55 g/2 oz chopped walnuts, to garnish (optional)

dressing

- 2 tbsp olive oil
- 1 tbsp walnut oil
- 2 tbsp lemon juice
- 1 tbsp chopped fresh mixed herbs, such as parsley and lemon thyme
- salt and pepper

1 Carve the chicken carefully, slicing the white meat. Divide the legs into thighs and drumsticks and trim the wings. Cover with clingfilm and refrigerate.

2 Put the cranberries in a bowl. Stir in the apple juice, cover with clingfilm and leave to soak for 30 minutes.

3 Meanwhile, blanch the sugar snap peas, refresh under cold running water and drain.

4 Peel, stone and slice the avocados, then toss in the lemon juice to prevent browning.

5 Separate the lettuce hearts and arrange on a large serving platter with the avocados, sugar snap peas, watercress, rocket and chicken.

6 Put all the dressing ingredients, with salt and pepper to taste, into a screw-top jar and shake well.

7 Drain the cranberries and mix them with the dressing, then pour over the salad.

8 Serve immediately, scattered with walnuts, if using.

waldorf salad

serves 4

- 500 g/1 lb 2 oz red apples, diced
- 3 tbsp lemon juice
- 150 ml/5 fl oz mayonnaise
- 1 head celery
- 4 shallots, sliced
- 1 garlic clove, crushed
- 85 g/3 oz chopped walnuts, plus extra to garnish
- 500 g/1 lb 2 oz lean cooked chicken, cubed
- 1 cos lettuce
- pepper

1 Place the apples in a bowl with the lemon juice and 1 tablespoon of the mayonnaise. Leave for 40 minutes or until required.

2 Slice the celery very thinly. Add the celery with the shallots, garlic and walnuts to the apples, mix and then add the remaining mayonnaise and blend thoroughly.

3 Add the chicken, season to taste with pepper and mix with the other ingredients.

4 Line a serving dish with the lettuce. Pile the chicken salad into the dish, garnish with chopped walnuts and serve.

cajun chicken salad

serves 4

- 4 skinless, boneless chicken breasts, about 140 g/5 oz each
- 4 tsp Cajun seasoning
- 2 tsp sunflower oil
- 1 ripe mango, peeled, stoned and cut into thick slices
- 200 g/7 oz mixed salad leaves
- 1 red onion, halved and thinly sliced
- 175 g/6 oz cooked beetroot, diced
- 85 g/3 oz radishes, sliced
- 55 g/2 oz walnut halves
- 4 tbsp walnut oil
- 1–2 tsp Dijon mustard
- 1 tbsp lemon juice
- 2 tbsp sesame seeds
- salt and pepper

1 Make 3 diagonal slashes across each chicken breast. Put the chicken into a shallow dish and sprinkle all over with the Cajun seasoning. Cover and refrigerate for at least 30 minutes.

2 When ready to cook, brush a griddle pan with the oil. Heat over a high heat until very hot and a few drops of water sprinkled into the pan sizzle immediately. Add the chicken and cook for 7–8 minutes on each side, or until thoroughly cooked. If still slightly pink in the centre, cook a little longer. Remove the chicken and reserve.

3 Add the mango slices to the pan and cook for 2 minutes on each side. Remove and reserve.

4 Meanwhile, arrange the salad leaves in a serving bowl and scatter over the onion, beetroot, radishes and walnut halves.

5 Put the walnut oil, mustard, lemon juice and salt and pepper to taste in a screw-top jar and shake until well blended. Pour over the salad and sprinkle with the sesame seeds.

6 Cut the reserved chicken into thick slices. Arrange the chicken and reserved mango slices on top of the salad and serve immediately.

chicken & pancetta caesar salad

serves 2

- 12 thin smoked pancetta slices
- 225 g/8 oz skinless, boneless chicken breasts, cubed
- 1 garlic clove, crushed
- 3 tbsp olive oil
- 1 small rustic or ciabatta roll, cut into chunky cubes
- 1 small cos lettuce, chopped into large pieces
- fresh Parmesan cheese shavings, to serve

dressing

- 3 tbsp mayonnaise
- 2 tbsp soured cream
- 1 tbsp milk
- 1 garlic clove, crushed
- ½ tsp Dijon mustard
- 2 tbsp finely grated Parmesan cheese
- 2 anchovy fillets in oil, drained and finely chopped
- pepper

1 To make the dressing, place all the ingredients in a food processor or hand blender and process until smooth.

2 Heat a large non-stick frying pan and add the pancetta slices. Cook over a high heat for about 2 minutes until crisp and frazzled. Remove with a slotted spoon and drain on kitchen paper. Add the chicken to the pan and fry over a medium–high heat for 5–6 minutes until golden and cooked through. Remove and drain with the pancetta.

3 Add the garlic and oil to the pan and stir in the bread cubes. Fry over a high heat, turning frequently, for 2–3 minutes until crisp and golden.

4 Place the lettuce and dressing in a serving bowl and toss together thoroughly. Add the pancetta and chicken and toss in gently. Scatter over the garlic croûtons and Parmesan cheese shavings and serve immediately.

honey & chicken pasta salad

serves 4
- 250 g/9 oz dried fusilli pasta
- 2 tbsp olive oil
- 1 onion, thinly sliced
- 1 garlic clove, crushed
- 400 g/14 oz skinless, boneless chicken breast, thinly sliced
- 2 tbsp wholegrain mustard
- 2 tbsp clear honey
- 175 g/6 oz cherry tomatoes, halved
- handful of mizuna or rocket leaves
- fresh thyme leaves, to garnish

dressing
- 3 tbsp olive oil
- 1 tbsp sherry vinegar
- 2 tsp clear honey
- 1 tbsp fresh thyme leaves
- salt and pepper

1 To make the dressing, place all the ingredients in a small bowl and whisk together.

2 Bring a large saucepan of lightly salted water to the boil. Add the pasta and return to the boil. Cook for 10–12 minutes until just tender.

3 Meanwhile, heat the oil in a large frying pan. Add the onion and garlic and fry for 5 minutes. Add the chicken and cook, stirring frequently, for 3–4 minutes until just cooked through. Stir the mustard and honey into the pan and cook for a further 2–3 minutes until the chicken and onion are golden brown and sticky.

4 Drain the pasta and transfer to a serving bowl. Pour over the dressing and toss well. Stir in the chicken and onion and leave to cool.

5 Gently stir the tomatoes and mizuna into the pasta. Serve garnished with the thyme leaves.

layered chicken salad

serves 4

- 1 red pepper, halved and deseeded
- 1 green pepper, halved and deseeded
- 2 small courgettes, sliced
- 750 g/1 lb 10 oz new potatoes, cooked
- 1 small onion, thinly sliced
- 3 tomatoes, sliced
- 350 g/12 oz cooked chicken, sliced
- snipped fresh chives, to garnish

dressing

- 150 ml/5 fl oz natural yogurt
- 3 tbsp mayonnaise
- 1 tbsp snipped fresh chives
- salt and pepper

1 Preheat the grill to high. Place the pepper halves skin side up, and grill until the skins blacken and begin to char. Remove the peppers with tongs, place in a bowl and cover with clingfilm. Set aside until cool enough to handle, then peel off the skins and slice the flesh.

2 Bring a small pan of lightly salted water to the boil. Add the courgettes, bring back to the boil and simmer for 3 minutes. Drain, rinse under cold running water to prevent any further cooking and drain again. Set aside.

3 To make the dressing, whisk together the yogurt, mayonnaise and snipped chives in a small bowl until well blended. Season to taste with salt and pepper.

4 Slice the potatoes, add them to the dressing and mix gently to coat evenly. Spoon the potatoes onto 4 serving plates, dividing them equally.

5 Top each plate with one quarter of the pepper slices and courgettes. Layer one quarter of the onion and tomato slices, then the sliced chicken, on top of each serving. Garnish with snipped chives and serve immediately.

chicken & cheese salad

serves 4

- 150 g/5½ oz rocket leaves
- 2 celery sticks, trimmed and sliced
- ½ cucumber, sliced
- 2 spring onions, trimmed and sliced
- 2 tbsp chopped fresh flat-leaf parsley
- 25 g/1 oz walnut pieces
- 350 g/12 oz boneless roast chicken, sliced
- 125 g/4½ oz Stilton cheese, cubed
- handful of seedless red grapes, halved (optional)
- salt and pepper

dressing

- 2 tbsp olive oil
- 1 tbsp sherry vinegar
- 1 tsp Dijon mustard
- 1 tbsp chopped mixed herbs

1 Wash the rocket leaves, pat dry with kitchen paper and put them into a large salad bowl. Add the celery, cucumber, spring onions, parsley and walnuts and mix together well. Transfer onto a large serving platter. Arrange the chicken slices over the salad, then scatter over the cheese. Add the red grapes, if using. Season well with salt and pepper.

2 To make the dressing, put all the ingredients into a small screw-top jar and shake until well blended. Drizzle the dressing over the salad and serve.

roast chicken with pesto cream salad

serves 6–8

- 600 g / 1 lb 5 oz skinless, boneless cooked chicken, cut into bite-sized pieces
- 3 celery sticks, chopped
- 2 large skinned red peppers from a jar, well drained and sliced
- salt and pepper
- iceberg lettuce leaves, to serve

pesto cream

- 150 ml / 5 fl oz crème fraîche or soured cream
- about 4 tbsp bottled pesto sauce

1 To make the pesto cream, put the crème fraîche into a large bowl, then beat in the pesto sauce. Taste and add more pesto if you want a stronger flavour.

2 Add the chicken, celery and red peppers to the bowl and gently toss together. Add salt and pepper to taste and toss again. Cover and chill until required.

3 Remove the salad from the fridge 10 minutes before serving to return to room temperature. Give the salad ingredients a good stir, then divide between individual plates lined with lettuce leaves.

Mmmm...
lunches & light bites

mediterranean pan bagna

serves 6–8

- 1 garlic clove, halved
- 1 large baguette, cut lengthways
- 4 tbsp olive oil
- 140 g/5 oz cold roast chicken, thinly sliced
- 2 large tomatoes, sliced
- 20 g/¾ oz canned anchovy fillets, drained
- 8 large stoned black olives, chopped
- pepper

1 Rub the garlic over the cut side of the bread and sprinkle with the oil.

2 Arrange the chicken on top of the bread. Arrange the tomatoes and anchovies on top of the chicken.

3 Scatter with the black olives and season with plenty of pepper. Sandwich the loaf back together and wrap tightly in foil until required. Cut into slices to serve.

open chicken sandwiches

serves 6–8

- 3 hard-boiled eggs, the yolks mashed and the whites chopped
- 25 g/1 oz butter, softened
- 2 tbsp English mustard
- 1 tsp anchovy essence
- 250 g/9 oz Cheddar cheese, grated
- 3 cooked skinless, boneless chicken breasts, diced
- 6 thick slices of rustic bread, buttered
- 12 slices each of tomato and cucumber
- pepper

1 In a large bowl, mix the egg yolks and whites with the softened butter, English mustard and anchovy essence and season to taste with pepper.

2 Mix in the Cheddar and chicken and spread the mixture on the bread.

3 Arrange the tomato and cucumber slices on top of the egg and chicken mixture and serve.

smoked chicken & ham focaccia

serves 2–4

- 1 thick focaccia loaf (about 15–17.5 cm/6–7 inches)
- handful of basil leaves
- 2 small courgettes, coarsely grated
- 6 wafer-thin slices of smoked chicken
- 6 wafer-thin slices of cooked ham
- 225 g/8 oz Taleggio cheese, cut into strips
- freshly grated nutmeg (optional)
- cherry tomatoes, to serve

1 Preheat a griddle plate or pan under the grill until both grill and griddle are hot. If you do not have a griddle or grill pan, heat a heavy baking sheet or roasting tin instead. Slice the focaccia in half horizontally and cut the top half into strips lengthways.

2 Cover the bottom half of the focaccia with basil leaves, top with the courgettes in an even layer and then cover with the chicken and ham, alternating the slices and wrinkling them. Lay the strips of focaccia on top, placing strips of Taleggio cheese between them. Sprinkle with a little nutmeg, if using.

3 Place the assembled bread on the hot griddle and cook under the grill, well away from the heat, for about 5 minutes, until the taleggio has melted and the top of the bread is browned. Serve immediately with cherry tomatoes, cutting the bread into four across the strips.

chicken & mushroom pizza

serves 2–4

- 4 tbsp olive oil, plus extra for brushing
- 2 shallots, thinly sliced
- 1 yellow pepper, deseeded and cut into thin strips
- 115 g/4 oz chestnut mushrooms, thinly sliced
- 350 g/12 oz skinless, boneless chicken breast portions, cut into thin strips
- 1 x 25-cm/10-inch pizza base
- 2 tbsp chopped fresh parsley
- 175 g/6 oz mozzarella cheese, grated
- salt and pepper

1 Preheat the oven to 200°C/400°F/Gas Mark 6. Brush a baking sheet with oil.

2 Heat 2 tablespoons of olive oil in a wok or large frying pan. Add the shallots, yellow pepper, mushrooms and chicken, and stir-fry over a medium-high heat for 4–5 minutes. Remove the mixture with a slotted spoon and leave to cool.

3 Brush the pizza base with 1 tablespoon of olive oil. Stir the parsley into the chicken and mushroom mixture and season with salt and pepper. Spread the mixture evenly over the pizza base almost to the edge. Sprinkle with the mozzarella, drizzle over the remaining olive oil, and bake for 20 minutes, until the edge is crisp and golden. Serve immediately.

chicken wraps

serves 4

- 150 g/5½ oz natural yogurt
- 1 tbsp wholegrain mustard
- 280 g/10 oz cooked skinless, boneless chicken breast, diced
- 140 g/5 oz iceberg lettuce, finely shredded
- 85 g/3 oz cucumber, thinly sliced
- 2 celery sticks, sliced
- 85 g/3 oz black seedless grapes, halved
- 8 x 20-cm/8-inch soft flour tortillas or 4 x 25-cm/10-inch soft flour tortillas
- pepper

1 Combine the yogurt and mustard in a bowl and season to taste with pepper. Stir in the chicken and toss until thoroughly coated.

2 Put the lettuce, cucumber, celery and grapes into a separate bowl and mix well.

3 Fold a tortilla in half and in half again to make a cone that is easy to hold. Half-fill the tortilla pocket with the salad mixture and top with some of the chicken mixture. Repeat with the remaining tortillas, salad and chicken. Serve immediately.

chicken fajitas

serves 4
- 3 tbsp olive oil, plus extra for drizzling
- 3 tbsp maple syrup or clear honey
- 1 tbsp red wine vinegar
- 2 garlic cloves, crushed
- 2 tsp dried oregano
- 1–2 tsp dried chilli flakes
- 4 skinless, boneless chicken breasts
- 2 red peppers, deseeded and cut into 2.5-cm/1-inch strips
- salt and pepper
- warmed flour tortillas and shredded lettuce, to serve

1 Place the oil, maple syrup, vinegar, garlic, oregano, chilli flakes and salt and pepper to taste in a large, shallow dish or bowl and mix together.

2 Slice the chicken across the grain into slices 2.5 cm/1 inch thick. Toss in the marinade until well coated. Cover and leave to chill in the refrigerator for 2–3 hours, turning occasionally.

3 Heat a griddle pan until hot. Lift the chicken slices from the marinade with a slotted spoon, lay on the griddle pan and cook over a medium–high heat for 3–4 minutes on each side, or until cooked through. Remove the chicken to a warmed plate and keep warm.

4 Add the peppers, skin side down, to the griddle pan and cook for 2 minutes on each side. Transfer to the plate.

5 Divide the chicken and peppers between the flour tortillas, top with a little shredded lettuce, wrap and serve immediately.

the ultimate chicken burger

serves 4
- 4 large skinless, boneless chicken breasts
- 1 large egg white
- 1 tbsp cornflour
- 1 tbsp plain flour
- 1 egg, beaten
- 55 g/2 oz fresh white breadcrumbs
- 2 tbsp sunflower oil
- 2 beef tomatoes, sliced

to serve
- 4 burger buns, sliced
- shredded lettuce
- mayonnaise

1 Place the chicken breasts between 2 sheets of non-stick baking parchment and flatten slightly using a meat mallet or a rolling pin. Beat the egg white and cornflour together, then brush over the chicken. Cover and leave to chill for 30 minutes, then coat in the plain flour.

2 Place the egg and breadcrumbs in 2 separate bowls and coat the burgers first in the egg, allowing any excess to drip back into the bowl, then in the breadcrumbs.

3 Heat a heavy-based frying pan and add the oil. When hot, add the burgers and cook over a medium heat for 6–8 minutes on each side, or until thoroughly cooked. Add the tomato slices for the last 1–2 minutes of the cooking time to heat through.

4 Serve the burgers in the burger buns with the tomato slices, a little shredded lettuce and a spoonful of mayonnaise.

bacon-wrapped chicken burgers

serves 4
- 450 g/1 lb fresh chicken mince
- 1 onion, grated
- 2 garlic cloves, crushed
- 55 g/2 oz pine kernels, toasted
- 55 g/2 oz Gruyère cheese, grated
- 2 tbsp fresh snipped chives
- 2 tbsp wholemeal flour
- 8 slices lean back bacon
- 1–2 tbsp sunflower oil
- salt and pepper

to serve
- 4 crusty rolls, sliced
- sliced red onion
- chopped lettuce
- mayonnaise
- chopped spring onions

1 Place the chicken mince, onion, garlic, pine kernels, Gruyère cheese, chives and salt and pepper in a food processor. Using the pulse button, blend the mixture together using short, sharp bursts. Scrape out onto a board and shape into 4 even-sized burgers. Coat in the flour, then cover and chill for 1 hour.

2 Wrap each burger with 2 bacon slices, securing in place with a wooden cocktail stick.

3 Heat a heavy-based frying pan and add the oil. When hot, add the burgers and cook over a medium heat for 5–6 minutes on each side, or until thoroughly cooked through.

4 Serve the burgers in the crusty rolls with sliced red onion, chopped lettuce, a spoonful of mayonnaise and chopped spring onions.

chicken nuggets

serves 4

- 3 skinless, boneless chicken breasts
- 4 tbsp wholemeal plain flour
- 1 tbsp wheatgerm
- ½ tsp ground cumin
- ½ tsp ground coriander
- 1 egg, lightly beaten
- 2 tbsp olive oil
- pepper

dipping sauce

- 100 g/3½ oz sunblush tomatoes
- 100 g/3½ oz fresh tomatoes, peeled, deseeded and chopped
- 2 tbsp mayonnaise

1 Preheat the oven to 190°C/375°F/Gas Mark 5. Cut the chicken breasts into 4-cm/1½-inch chunks. Mix the flour, wheatgerm, cumin, coriander, and pepper to taste, in a bowl, then divide in half and put on 2 separate plates. Put the beaten egg on a third plate.

2 Pour the oil into a baking tray and heat in the oven. Roll the chicken pieces in one plate of flour, shake to remove any excess, then roll in the egg and in the second plate of flour, again shaking off any excess flour. When all the nuggets are ready, remove the baking tray from the oven and toss the nuggets in the hot oil. Roast in the oven for 25–30 minutes until golden and crisp.

3 Meanwhile, to make the dipping sauce, put both kinds of tomatoes in a blender or food processor and process until smooth. Add the mayonnaise and process again until well combined.

4 Remove the nuggets from the oven and drain on kitchen paper. Serve with the dipping sauce.

jerk chicken

serves 4

- 2 fresh red chillies
- 2 tbsp corn oil, plus extra for brushing
- 2 garlic cloves, finely chopped
- 1 tbsp finely chopped onion
- 1 tbsp finely chopped spring onion
- 1 tbsp white wine vinegar
- 1 tbsp lime juice
- 2 tsp demerara sugar
- 1 tsp dried thyme
- 1 tsp ground cinnamon
- 1 tsp ground mixed spice
- ¼ tsp freshly grated nutmeg
- 4 chicken quarters
- salt and pepper
- sprigs of fresh coriander and lime wedges, to garnish

1 Deseed and finely chop the red chillies, then place them in a small glass bowl with the oil, garlic, onion, spring onion, vinegar, lime juice, sugar, thyme, cinnamon, mixed spice and nutmeg. Season to taste with salt and pepper and mash thoroughly with a fork.

2 Using a sharp knife, make a series of diagonal slashes in the chicken pieces and place them in a large, shallow, non-metallic dish. Spoon the jerk seasoning over the chicken, rubbing it well into the slashes. Cover and leave to marinate in the refrigerator for up to 8 hours.

3 Preheat the grill. Remove the chicken from the marinade, discarding the marinade, brush with oil and cook under the preheated grill, turning frequently, for 30–35 minutes. Transfer to plates and serve garnished with sprigs of coriander and lime wedges.

mustard & honey drumsticks

serves 4
- 8 chicken drumsticks
- sprigs of fresh parsley, to garnish

glaze
- 125 ml/4 fl oz clear honey
- 4 tbsp Dijon mustard
- 4 tbsp wholegrain mustard
- 4 tbsp white wine vinegar
- 2 tbsp sunflower oil
- salt and pepper

1 Using a sharp knife, make 2–3 diagonal slashes in the chicken drumsticks and place them in a large, non-metallic dish.

2 Mix together all the ingredients for the glaze in a jug and season to taste with salt and pepper. Pour the glaze over the drumsticks, turning until the drumsticks are well coated. Cover with clingfilm and leave to marinate in the refrigerator for at least 1 hour.

3 Preheat the grill. Drain the chicken drumsticks, reserving the marinade. Cook the chicken under the preheated grill, turning frequently and brushing with the reserved marinade, for 25–30 minutes, or until thoroughly cooked. Transfer to serving plates, garnish with sprigs of parsley and serve immediately.

chicken croquettes

serves 4

- 6 tbsp olive oil
- 1 onion, finely chopped
- 1 celery stick, finely chopped
- 225 g/8 oz cooked chicken, finely chopped
- 3 tomatoes
- 550 g/1 lb 4 oz boiled potatoes, finely chopped
- plain flour, for dusting
- 2 eggs, lightly beaten
- 115 g/4 oz dry breadcrumbs
- 1 tbsp chopped fresh parsley

rich tomato sauce

- 1 rasher lean bacon
- 25 g/1 oz butter
- 1 shallot, finely chopped
- 1 garlic clove, finely chopped
- 1 celery stick, finely chopped
- 1 carrot, finely chopped
- 400 g/14 oz canned chopped tomatoes
- 2 tsp cornflour
- 300 ml/10 fl oz chicken stock
- salt and pepper

1 Heat half the oil in a saucepan. Add the onion and celery and cook over a low heat, stirring occasionally, for 5 minutes, until softened. Add the chicken, tomatoes and potatoes and cook, stirring frequently, for 8–10 minutes. Transfer the mixture to a food processor and process until smooth. Scrape into a bowl and leave to cool, then chill for 1 hour.

2 Meanwhile, make the sauce. Remove the bacon rind and dice the bacon. Melt the butter with the bacon rind in a saucepan. Add the bacon, shallot, garlic, celery and carrot and cook over a low heat, stirring occasionally, for 5 minutes. Stir in the tomatoes and cook, stirring occasionally, for 5 minutes. Stir the cornflour into the stock and pour it into the pan. Season to taste with salt and pepper. Cover and simmer, stirring occasionally, for 20 minutes, until thickened. Remove and discard the bacon rind.

3 Lightly dust your hands with flour and divide the chicken mixture into 8–12 pieces. Roll each into a small croquette. Place the eggs in a shallow bowl and spread out the breadcrumbs in a separate shallow bowl. Dip the croquettes into the beaten egg, then into the breadcrumbs to coat.

4 Heat the remaining oil in a frying pan. Add the croquettes and cook over a medium heat, turning once, for 10 minutes. Drain on kitchen paper. Pour the sauce over the croquettes, sprinkle with the parsley and serve immediately.

chicken & chilli enchiladas

serves 4

- corn oil, for brushing
- 5 fresh hot green chillies, such as jalapeño, deseeded and chopped
- 1 Spanish onion, chopped
- 2 garlic cloves, chopped
- 2 tbsp chopped fresh coriander
- 2 tbsp lime juice
- 125 ml/4 fl oz chicken stock
- 2 beef tomatoes, peeled, deseeded and chopped
- pinch of sugar
- 350 g/12 oz cooked chicken, shredded
- 85 g/3 oz queso anejo or Cheddar cheese, grated
- 2 tsp chopped fresh oregano
- 8 corn or flour tortillas
- salt

1 Preheat the oven to 180°C/350°F/Gas Mark 4 and brush a large, ovenproof dish with oil. Place two-thirds of the chillies, the onion, garlic, coriander, lime juice, stock, tomatoes and sugar in a food processor and pulse to a purée. Scrape into a saucepan and simmer over a medium heat for 10 minutes, until thickened.

2 Mix together the remaining chillies, the chicken, 55 g/2 oz of the cheese and the oregano. Season with salt and stir in half the sauce.

3 Heat the tortillas in a dry, heavy-based frying pan or in the microwave according to the packet instructions. Divide the chicken mixture between them, spooning it along the centres, then roll up and place, seam-side down, in the dish.

4 Pour the remaining sauce over the enchiladas and sprinkle with the remaining cheese. Bake in the preheated oven for 20 minutes and serve hot.

zesty chicken kebabs

serves 6-8

- 4 skinless, boneless chicken breasts, about 175 g/6 oz each
- finely grated rind and juice of ½ lemon
- finely grated rind and juice of ½ orange
- 2 tbsp clear honey
- 2 tbsp olive oil
- 2 tbsp chopped fresh mint
- ¼ tsp ground coriander
- salt and pepper

1 Using a sharp knife, cut the chicken into 2.5-cm/ 1-inch cubes, then place in a large glass bowl. Place the lemon and orange rind, the lemon and orange juice, the honey, oil, mint and coriander in a jug and mix together. Season to taste with salt and pepper. Pour the marinade over the chicken and toss until they are thoroughly coated. Cover with clingfilm and leave to marinate in the refrigerator for up to 8 hours.

2 Preheat the barbecue or grill. Drain the chicken, reserving the marinade. Thread the chicken onto 8 metal or pre-soaked wooden skewers.

3 Cook the skewers over medium–hot coals or under the preheated grill, turning and basting frequently with the reserved marinade, for 6–10 minutes, or until cooked through. Transfer to a large serving plate and serve immediately.

cajun chicken

serves 4
- 4 chicken drumsticks
- 4 chicken thighs
- 2 fresh sweetcorn cobs, husks and silks removed
- 85 g/3 oz butter, melted
- fresh flat-leaf parsley sprigs, to garnish

spice mix
- 2 tsp onion powder
- 2 tsp paprika
- 1½ tsp salt
- 1 tsp garlic powder
- 1 tsp dried thyme
- 1 tsp cayenne pepper
- 1 tsp ground black pepper
- ½ tsp ground white pepper
- ¼ tsp ground cumin

1 Preheat the barbecue or grill. Using a sharp knife, make 2–3 diagonal slashes in the chicken drumsticks and thighs, then place them in a large dish. Cut the sweetcorn cobs into thick slices and add them to the dish. Mix together all the ingredients for the spice mix in a small bowl.

2 Brush the chicken and sweetcorn with the melted butter and sprinkle with the spice mix. Toss to coat well.

3 Cook the chicken over medium–hot coals or under the preheated grill, turning occasionally, for 15 minutes, then add the sweetcorn slices and cook, turning occasionally, for a further 10–15 minutes, or until beginning to blacken slightly at the edges. Transfer to a large serving plate, garnish with the parsley and serve immediately.

chicken kiev

serves 6–8

- 115 g/4 oz butter, softened
- 3–4 garlic cloves, very finely chopped
- 1 tbsp chopped fresh parsley
- 1 tbsp snipped fresh chives
- finely grated rind and juice of ½ lemon
- 8 skinless, boneless chicken breasts, about 115 g/4 oz each
- 55 g/2 oz plain flour
- 2 eggs, lightly beaten
- 175 g/6 oz dry breadcrumbs
- groundnut or sunflower oil, for deep-frying
- salt and pepper

1 Beat the butter in a bowl with the garlic, herbs, lemon rind and juice. Season to taste with salt and pepper. Divide into 8 pieces, then shape into cylinders. Wrap in foil and chill for about 2 hours, until firm.

2 Place the chicken between 2 sheets of clingfilm. Pound gently with a rolling pin to flatten the chicken to an even thickness. Place a butter cylinder on each chicken piece and roll up. Secure with cocktail sticks.

3 Place the flour, eggs and breadcrumbs in separate shallow dishes. Dip the rolls into the flour, then the egg and, finally, the breadcrumbs. Place on a plate, cover and chill for 1 hour.

4 Heat the oil in a saucepan or deep-fat fryer to 180°C/350°F or until a cube of bread browns in 30 seconds. Deep-fry the chicken in batches for 8–10 minutes, or until cooked through and golden brown. Drain on kitchen paper. Serve immediately.

spicy chicken & tomato kebabs

serves 4
- 500 g/1 lb 2 oz skinless, boneless chicken breasts
- 3 tbsp tomato purée
- 2 tbsp clear honey
- 2 tbsp Worcestershire sauce
- 1 tbsp chopped fresh rosemary
- 250 g/9 oz cherry tomatoes

1 Using a sharp knife, cut the chicken into small chunks and place in a bowl. Mix together the tomato purée, honey, Worcestershire sauce and rosemary in a separate bowl, then add to the chicken, stirring to coat evenly.

2 Preheat the barbecue or grill. Drain the chicken, reserving the marinade. Thread the chicken pieces and cherry tomatoes alternately onto 8 metal or pre-soaked wooden skewers.

3 Cook the kebabs over medium–hot coals or under the preheated grill, turning occasionally and basting with the reserved marinade, for 8–10 minutes, until the chicken is cooked through. Transfer to a large plate and serve immediately.

chicken with tarragon butter

serves 4
- 4 skinless, boneless chicken breasts, about 225 g/8 oz each
- oil, for greasing

tarragon butter
- 100 g/3½ oz unsalted butter, at room temperature
- 5 tbsp chopped fresh tarragon
- 1 shallot, finely chopped
- salt and pepper

marinade
- 1½ tbsp lemon juice
- 2 tbsp water
- 1 tsp sugar
- 1 tsp salt
- ½ tsp pepper
- 3 tbsp olive oil

1 Preheat the barbecue. To make the tarragon butter, mash the butter with a fork until soft, then add the tarragon, shallot and salt and pepper to taste, mixing well. Scrape the mixture onto a piece of clingfilm and form into a log. Wrap tightly and chill in the refrigerator.

2 Slice the chicken breasts lengthways to make 8 portions. Place in a single layer in a shallow dish. Mix together the marinade ingredients and pour over the chicken. Cover with clingfilm and leave to marinate in the refrigerator for 30 minutes, turning halfway through.

3 Drain the chicken, discarding the marinade. Pat dry and lightly brush with oil. Grease the grill rack. Place the chicken on the rack and cover with a disposable foil tray. Grill over medium–hot coals for 5–6 minutes, until the underside is striped with grill marks and is no longer translucent. Using tongs, turn and cook the other side for 4–5 minutes, or until cooked through.

4 Place in a warmed dish, cover with foil and leave to rest in a warm place for 5 minutes. Serve immediately with slices of the tarragon butter.

yaki soba

serves 2

- 400 g/14 oz ramen noodles
- 1 onion, finely sliced
- 200 g/7 oz beansprouts
- 1 red pepper, deseeded and sliced
- 150 g/5½ oz chicken, cooked and sliced
- 12 cooked peeled prawns
- 1 tbsp oil, for stir-frying
- 2 tbsp shoyu
- ½ tbsp mirin
- 1 tsp sesame oil
- 1 tsp sesame seeds
- 2 spring onions, finely sliced

1 Cook the noodles according to the packet instructions, drain well, and tip into a bowl.

2 Mix the onion, beansprouts, red pepper, chicken and prawns together in a bowl. Stir through the noodles. Meanwhile, preheat a wok over high heat, add the oil and heat until very hot.

3 Add the noodle mixture and stir-fry for 4 minutes, or until golden, then add the shoyu, mirin and sesame oil and toss together.

4 Divide the noodles between two bowls. Sprinkle with sesame seeds and spring onions and serve.

chicken fried rice

serves 4

- ½ tbsp sesame oil
- 6 shallots, peeled and cut into quarters
- 450 g/1 lb cooked chicken, cubed
- 3 tbsp soy sauce
- 2 carrots, diced
- 1 celery stick, diced
- 1 red pepper, deseeded and diced
- 175 g/6 oz fresh peas
- 100 g/3½ oz canned sweetcorn, drained
- 275 g/9¾ oz cooked long-grain rice
- 2 large eggs

1 Heat the oil in a preheated wok or large frying pan over a medium heat.

2 Add the shallots and fry until soft, then add the chicken and 2 tablespoons of the soy sauce and stir-fry for 5–6 minutes.

3 Stir in the carrots, celery, red pepper, peas and sweetcorn and stir-fry for a further 5 minutes.

4 Add the rice and stir thoroughly. Finally, beat the eggs and pour into the mixture. Stir until the eggs are beginning to set, then add in the remaining soy sauce.

5 Transfer to bowls and serve immediately.

sweet & sour chicken

serves 4-6

- 450 g/1 lb lean chicken, cubed
- 5 tbsp vegetable or groundnut oil
- ½ tsp crushed garlic
- ½ tsp finely chopped fresh ginger
- 1 green pepper, deseeded and roughly chopped
- 1 onion, roughly chopped
- 1 carrot, finely sliced
- 1 tsp sesame oil
- 1 tbsp finely chopped spring onion
- freshly cooked plain rice, to serve

marinade

- 2 tsp light soy sauce
- 1 tsp Chinese rice wine
- pinch of white pepper
- ½ tsp salt
- dash of sesame oil

sauce

- 8 tbsp rice vinegar
- 4 tbsp sugar
- 2 tsp light soy sauce
- 6 tbsp tomato ketchup

1 Combine all the marinade ingredients in a bowl and marinate the chicken for at least 20 minutes.

2 To prepare the sauce, heat the vinegar in a pan and add the sugar, soy sauce and tomato ketchup. Stir to dissolve the sugar, then set aside.

3 Heat a wok over a high heat, then add 3 tablespoons of the vegetable oil. Stir-fry the chicken until it starts to turn golden brown. Remove and set aside. Wipe the wok clean with kitchen paper.

4 Heat the wok over a high heat, and add the remaining vegetable oil and cook the garlic and ginger until fragrant. Add the vegetables and cook for 2 minutes. Add the chicken and cook for 1 minute. Finally, add the sauce and the sesame oil, then stir in the spring onion and serve immediately with rice.

chicken chow mein

serves 4

- 250 g/9 oz medium egg noodles
- 2 tbsp sunflower oil
- 275 g/9¾ oz cooked chicken breasts, shredded
- 1 garlic clove, finely chopped
- 1 red pepper, deseeded and thinly sliced
- 100 g/3½ oz shiitake mushrooms, sliced
- 6 spring onions, sliced
- 100 g/3½ oz beansprouts
- 3 tbsp soy sauce
- 1 tbsp sesame oil

1 Place the egg noodles in a large bowl or dish and break them up slightly. Pour enough boiling water over the noodles to cover and leave to stand whilst preparing the other ingredients.

2 Heat the sunflower oil in a large preheated wok. Add the chicken, garlic, red pepper, mushrooms, spring onions and beansprouts to the wok and stir-fry for about 5 minutes.

3 Drain the noodles thoroughly. Add the noodles to the wok, toss well and stir-fry for a further 5 minutes.

4 Drizzle the soy sauce and sesame oil over the chow mein and toss until well combined.

5 Transfer to warmed serving bowls and serve immediately.

chicken with pak cho

serves 4

- 175 g/6 oz broccoli
- 1 tbsp peanut oil
- 2.5-cm/1-inch piece fresh ginger, finely grated
- 1 fresh red Thai chilli, deseeded and chopped
- 2 garlic cloves, crushed
- 1 red onion, cut into wedges
- 450 g/1 lb skinless, boneless chicken breast, cut into thin strips
- 175 g/6 oz pak choi, shredded
- 115 g/4 oz baby corn, halved
- 1 tbsp light soy sauce
- 1 tbsp Thai fish sauce
- 1 tbsp chopped fresh coriander
- 1 tbsp toasted sesame seeds

1 Break the broccoli into small florets and cook in a saucepan of lightly salted boiling water for 3 minutes. Drain and set aside.

2 Heat a wok over a high heat until almost smoking, add the oil, then add the ginger, chilli and garlic. Stir-fry for 1 minute. Add the onion and chicken and stir-fry for a further 3–4 minutes, or until the chicken is sealed on all sides.

3 Add the remaining vegetables to the wok, including the broccoli, and stir-fry for 3–4 minutes, or until tender.

4 Add the soy and Thai fish sauces to the wok and stir-fry for a further 1–2 minutes, then serve at once, sprinkled with the coriander and sesame seeds.

quick chicken laksa

serves 4

- 850 ml/1½ pints canned coconut milk
- 200 ml/7 fl oz chicken stock
- 2–3 tbsp laksa paste
- 3 skinless, boneless chicken breasts, about 175 g/6 oz each, sliced into strips
- 250 g/9 oz cherry tomatoes, halved
- 250 g/9 oz sugar snap peas, halved diagonally
- 200 g/7 oz dried rice noodles
- 1 bunch fresh coriander, roughly chopped

1 Pour the coconut milk and stock into a saucepan and stir in the laksa paste. Add the chicken strips and simmer for 10–15 minutes over a gentle heat until the chicken is cooked through.

2 Stir in the tomatoes, sugar snap peas and noodles. Simmer for a further 2–3 minutes. Stir in the coriander and serve immediately.

cross the bridge noodles

serves 4

- 300 g/10½ oz dried fine egg noodles or rice sticks
- 200 g/7 oz choi sum or similar green vegetable
- 2 litres/3½ pints chicken stock
- 1-cm/½-inch piece fresh ginger, peeled
- 1–2 tsp salt
- 1 tsp sugar
- 1 boneless, skinless chicken breast, finely sliced diagonally
- 200 g/7 oz white fish fillet, finely sliced diagonally
- 1 tbsp light soy sauce

1 Cook the noodles according to the instructions on the packet. When cooked, rinse under cold water and set aside. Blanch the choi sum in a large saucepan of boiling water for 30 seconds. Rinse under cold water and set aside.

2 In a large saucepan, bring the stock to the boil, then add the ginger, 1 teaspoon of the salt and the sugar and skim the surface. Add the chicken and cook for about 4 minutes, then add the fish and simmer for a further 4 minutes, or until the fish and chicken are cooked through.

3 Add the noodles and choi sum with the light soy sauce and bring back to the boil. Taste and adjust the seasoning if necessary. Serve immediately in large individual noodle bowls.

Mmmm...
weekday meals

chicken & autumn vegetable bake

serves 4

- 3 tbsp olive oil
- 2 leeks, sliced
- 2 garlic cloves, sliced
- 2 large chicken breasts, about 175 g/6 oz each, cut into bite-sized pieces
- 2 sweet potatoes, peeled and cut into chunks
- 2 parsnips, scrubbed and sliced
- 1 red pepper, deseeded and cut into strips
- 1 yellow pepper, deseeded and cut into strips
- 250 g/9 oz mixed wild mushrooms, cleaned
- 400 g/14 oz tomatoes, roughly chopped
- 300 g/10½ oz cooked white long-grain rice
- 1 small bunch fresh parsley, chopped
- 125 g/4½ oz mature Cheddar cheese, grated
- salt and pepper
- salad, to serve (optional)

1 Preheat the oven to 180°C/350°F/Gas Mark 4.

2 Heat the oil in a large frying pan over a medium heat, add the leeks and garlic and cook, stirring frequently, for 3–4 minutes until softened. Add the chicken and cook, stirring frequently, for 5 minutes. Add the sweet potatoes and parsnips and cook, stirring frequently, for 5 minutes, or until golden and beginning to soften. Add the peppers and mushrooms and cook, stirring frequently, for 5 minutes. Stir in the tomatoes, rice and parsley and season to taste with salt and pepper.

3 Spoon the mixture into an ovenproof dish, scatter over the Cheddar cheese and bake in the preheated oven for 20–25 minutes. Serve immediately with a salad, if desired.

chicken, potato & leek pie

serves 4

- 225 g/8 oz waxy potatoes, cubed
- 5 tbsp butter
- 1 skinless, boneless chicken breast, about 175 g/6 oz, cubed
- 1 leek, sliced
- 150 g/5½ oz chestnut mushrooms, sliced
- 2½ tbsp plain flour
- 300 ml/10 fl oz milk
- 1 tbsp Dijon mustard
- 2 tbsp chopped fresh sage
- 225 g/8 oz filo pastry, thawed if frozen
- 3 tbsp melted butter
- salt and pepper

1 Preheat the oven to 180°C/350°F/Gas Mark 4. Cook the potato cubes in a saucepan of boiling water for 5 minutes. Drain and set aside.

2 Melt the butter in a frying pan and cook the chicken cubes for 5 minutes or until browned all over.

3 Add the leek and mushrooms and cook for 3 minutes, stirring. Stir in the flour and cook for 1 minute stirring constantly. Gradually stir in the milk and bring to the boil. Add the mustard, sage and reserved potato cubes and simmer for 10 minutes. Season to taste with salt and pepper.

4 Meanwhile, line a deep pie dish with half of the filo pastry. Spoon the filling into the dish and cover with 1 sheet of pastry. Brush the pastry with butter and lay another sheet on top. Brush this sheet with butter.

5 Cut the remaining filo pastry into strips and fold them onto the top of the pie to create a ruffled effect. Brush the strips with the melted butter and cook in the preheated oven for 45 minutes or until golden brown and crisp. Serve hot.

classic chicken pie with cinnamon

serves 4–6

- 2–3 tbsp olive oil
- 100 g/3½ oz butter
- 3 onions, halved lengthways, then halved crossways and sliced with the grain
- 2 garlic cloves, chopped
- 2–3 tbsp blanched almonds, chopped
- 1–2 tsp ground cinnamon, plus extra for dusting
- 1 tsp ground ginger
- 1 tsp paprika
- 1 tsp ground coriander
- 250 g/9 oz chicken breast fillets, cut into bite-sized pieces
- 1 bunch of fresh flat-leaf parsley, finely chopped
- 1 large bunch of fresh coriander, finely chopped
- 7–8 sheets filo pastry, thawed if frozen
- 1 egg yolk, mixed with 1 tsp water
- salt and pepper

1 Preheat the oven to 200°C/400°F/Gas Mark 6. Heat the oil in a heavy-based frying pan with a knob of the butter, add the onions and cook over a medium heat, stirring frequently, for 2–3 minutes.

2 Stir in the garlic and almonds and cook for 2 minutes, stirring, then add the spices. Add the chicken and cook gently for 3–4 minutes, or until all the liquid in the pan has evaporated. Add the herbs, season to taste and leave to cool.

3 Melt the remaining butter in a small saucepan. Separate the sheets of pastry and keep covered with a clean, damp tea towel. Brush a little melted butter over the base of a round ovenproof dish and cover with a sheet of pastry, allowing the sides to flop over the edge. Brush the pastry with melted butter and place another sheet on top. Repeat with another two layers.

4 Spread the chicken and onion mixture on top of the pastry and fold the edges over the filling. Cover with the remaining sheets of pastry, brushing each one with butter. Tuck the overlapping edges under the pie. Brush the egg yolk mixture over the top of the pie to glaze. Bake in the preheated oven for 25 minutes, or until the pastry is puffed up and golden. Dust the top with cinnamon and serve immediately.

chicken lasagne

serves 4–6

- 2 tbsp olive oil
- 1 large onion, finely chopped
- 500 g/1 lb 2 oz fresh chicken mince
- 100 g/3½ oz smoked pancetta, chopped
- 250 g/9 oz chestnut mushrooms, chopped
- 100 g/3½ oz dried porcini mushrooms, soaked
- 150 ml/5 fl oz dry white wine
- 400 g/14 oz canned chopped tomatoes
- 3 tbsp chopped fresh basil leaves
- 9 sheets dried lasagne
- 3 tbsp finely grated Parmesan cheese
- salt and pepper

white sauce

- 600 ml/1 pint milk
- 55 g/2 oz butter
- 55 g/2 oz plain flour
- 1 bay leaf

1 Preheat the oven to 190°C/375°F/Gas Mark 5. For the white sauce, heat the milk, butter, flour and bay leaf in a pan, whisking constantly, until smooth and thick. Season to taste with salt and pepper, cover and leave to stand.

2 Heat the oil in a large saucepan and fry the onion, stirring, for 3–4 minutes. Add the chicken and pancetta and cook for 6–8 minutes. Stir in both types of mushrooms and cook for a further 2–3 minutes. Add the wine and bring to the boil. Pour in the tomatoes, cover and simmer for 20 minutes. Stir in the basil.

3 Meanwhile, bring a large saucepan of lightly salted water to the boil. Add the lasagne sheets, bring back to the boil and cook according to the packet instructions. Drain well on a clean tea towel. Arrange 3 of the lasagne sheets in a rectangular ovenproof dish, then spoon over a third of the meat sauce.

4 Remove and discard the bay leaf from the white sauce. Spread a third of the sauce over the meat. Repeat the layers twice more, finishing with a layer of white sauce. Sprinkle with the Parmesan and bake in the preheated oven for 35–40 minutes, until the topping is golden brown and bubbling. Serve immediately.

chicken bake

serves 4

- 4 skinless, boneless chicken breasts
- 2 aubergines, sliced
- 4 tbsp plain flour
- 275 ml/9½ fl oz olive oil
- 55 g/2 oz dry breadcrumbs
- 1 egg
- 55 g/2 oz Parmesan cheese, grated
- chopped fresh flat-leaf parsley, to garnish

tomato sauce

- 25 g/1 oz butter
- 2 tbsp olive oil
- 1 onion, finely chopped
- 2 garlic cloves, finely chopped
- 1 celery stick, finely chopped
- 400 g/14 oz canned chopped tomatoes
- 2 tbsp tomato purée
- 6 stoned olives, sliced
- brown sugar, to taste
- 1 tsp dried oregano
- 100 ml/3½ fl oz water
- salt and pepper

1 Put the chicken between 2 sheets of clingfilm and beat until thin and even. Cut into 10-cm/4-inch pieces and set aside. To make the sauce, melt the butter with the oil in a saucepan. Add the onion, garlic and celery and cook over a low heat, stirring occasionally, for 5 minutes, until softened. Stir in the tomatoes, tomato purée, olives, sugar to taste, oregano and water and season to taste. Increase the heat to medium and bring to the boil, then reduce the heat and simmer, stirring occasionally, for 15–20 minutes, until thickened.

2 Meanwhile, dip the aubergine slices in the flour to coat. Heat 5 tablespoons of the oil in a large frying pan and cook the aubergine slices, in batches, for 3 minutes on each side, until lightly browned, adding more oil as necessary.

3 Preheat the oven to 180°C/350°F/Gas Mark 4. Spread out the breadcrumbs in a shallow dish and lightly beat the egg in a separate shallow dish. Dip the chicken first in the egg and then in the breadcrumbs to coat. Heat the remaining oil in the frying pan. Add the chicken and cook over a medium heat for 2 minutes on each side, until golden. Layer the chicken and aubergine slices in an ovenproof dish, pour over the sauce and sprinkle with the Parmesan. Bake in the preheated oven for 20 minutes, until golden. Garnish with parsley and serve immediately.

mediterranean chicken parcels

serves 6

- 1 tbsp olive oil
- 6 skinless, boneless chicken breasts
- 250 g/9 oz mozzarella cheese, sliced
- 500 g/1 lb 2 oz courgettes, sliced
- 6 large tomatoes, sliced
- 1 small bunch of fresh basil leaves, torn
- pepper

1 Preheat the oven to 200°C/400°F/Gas Mark 6. Cut 6 pieces of foil, each about 25 cm/10 inches square. Brush the foil squares lightly with oil and set aside until required.

2 With a sharp knife, slash each chicken breast at intervals, then place the mozzarella in the cuts in the chicken.

3 Divide the courgettes and tomatoes between the pieces of foil and season to taste with pepper. Scatter the basil over the vegetables in each parcel.

4 Place a chicken breast on top of each pile of vegetables, then wrap in the foil to enclose the chicken and vegetables, tucking in the ends.

5 Place on a baking tray and bake in the preheated oven for about 30 minutes.

6 To serve, unwrap each foil parcel and transfer the contents to warmed serving plates.

chicken breasts with a parmesan crumb topping

serves 4

- 4 skinless, boneless chicken breasts
- 5 tbsp pesto sauce
- 40 g/1½ oz ciabatta breadcrumbs
- 25 g/1 oz Parmesan cheese, grated
- finely grated rind of ½ lemon
- 2 tbsp olive oil
- salt and pepper
- roasted vine tomatoes, to serve

1 Preheat the oven to 220°C/425°F/Gas Mark 7. Cut a deep slash into each chicken breast to make a pocket.

2 Open out the chicken breasts and spread 1 tablespoon of the pesto into each pocket.

3 Fold the chicken flesh back over the pesto and place in an ovenproof dish.

4 Mix the remaining pesto with the breadcrumbs, Parmesan and lemon rind.

5 Spread the breadcrumb mixture over the chicken breasts. Season to taste with salt and pepper and drizzle with the oil.

6 Bake in the preheated oven for about 20 minutes, or until the juices run clear when a skewer is inserted into the thickest part of the meat.

7 Serve the chicken hot with roasted vine tomatoes.

chicken with tomato & cinnamon sauce

serves 4

- 55 g/2 oz butter
- 2 tbsp olive oil
- 4 chicken quarters
- 1 onion, finely chopped
- 2 garlic cloves, finely chopped
- 1 celery stick, finely chopped
- 400 g/14 oz canned chopped tomatoes
- 2 tbsp tomato purée
- 1 tsp Dijon mustard
- brown sugar, to taste
- 2 tbsp lemon juice
- 3 tbsp chicken stock
- 1 tsp dried oregano
- ¾ tsp ground cinnamon
- salt and pepper

1 Melt the butter with the oil in a flameproof casserole. Season the chicken well with salt and pepper, add to the casserole and cook over a medium heat, turning frequently, for 8–10 minutes, until evenly browned. Remove from the casserole and set aside.

2 Add the onion, garlic and celery to the casserole and cook over a low heat, stirring occasionally, for 5 minutes, until softened. Stir in the tomatoes, tomato purée, mustard, sugar to taste, lemon juice, stock, oregano and cinnamon and season to taste with salt and pepper. Increase the heat to medium and bring to the boil, then reduce the heat and simmer, stirring occasionally, for 15 minutes.

3 Return the chicken to the casserole and spoon the sauce over it. Cover and simmer, stirring occasionally, for 30 minutes, until the chicken is tender and cooked through. Serve immediately.

devilled chicken

serves 4

- 1 whole chicken, weighing 2.25 kg/5 lb
- 2 carrots, cut into chunks
- 1 celery stick, cut into lengths
- 6 black peppercorns
- 1 bouquet garni
- pinch of salt
- 25 g/1 oz butter, melted
- fresh thyme leaves, to garnish

devil sauce

- 25 g/1 oz butter
- 2 tbsp olive oil
- 2 shallots, finely chopped
- 2 garlic cloves, finely chopped
- 1 celery stick, finely chopped
- 400 g/14 oz canned chopped tomatoes
- 2 tbsp tomato purée
- brown sugar, to taste
- 3 tbsp Worcestershire sauce
- 1 tbsp lemon juice
- 2 tbsp tarragon vinegar
- 1 bay leaf
- salt and pepper

1 Put the chicken, carrots, celery, peppercorns, bouquet garni and salt into a large saucepan and pour in water to cover. Bring to the boil over a high heat, then reduce the heat, cover and simmer for 1½ hours, until tender and cooked through. Remove from the heat and leave to cool.

2 Meanwhile, make the sauce. Melt the butter with the oil in a saucepan. Add the shallots, garlic and celery and cook over a low heat, stirring occasionally, for 5 minutes, until softened. Stir in the tomatoes, tomato purée, sugar to taste, Worcestershire sauce, lemon juice, vinegar and bay leaf and season to taste with salt and pepper. Increase the heat to medium and bring to the boil, then reduce the heat and simmer, stirring occasionally, for 15–20 minutes, until thickened.

3 Preheat the grill. Remove the chicken from the pan and strain the cooking liquid into a bowl. Remove and discard the skin, cut the chicken into eight pieces and put them into a flameproof casserole. Brush the chicken with the melted butter and cook under the preheated grill for 8 minutes on each side, until evenly browned.

4 Remove and discard the bay leaf from the sauce and stir in 300 ml/10 fl oz of the reserved cooking liquid. Pour the sauce over the chicken and cook over a medium heat for 10–15 minutes, until the chicken is cooked through. Garnish with thyme and serve immediately.

fried chicken with tomato & bacon sauce

serves 4
- 25 g/1 oz butter
- 2 tbsp olive oil
- 4 skinless, boneless chicken breasts or 8 skinless, boneless chicken thighs

tomato & bacon sauce
- 25 g/1 oz butter
- 2 tbsp olive oil
- 1 large onion, finely chopped
- 2 garlic cloves, finely chopped
- 1 celery stick, finely chopped
- 4 rashers bacon, diced
- 400 g/14 oz canned chopped tomatoes
- 2 tbsp tomato purée
- brown sugar, to taste
- 100 ml/3½ fl oz water
- 1 tbsp chopped fresh basil
- 1 tbsp chopped fresh parsley, plus extra to garnish
- salt and pepper

1 First, make the sauce. Melt the butter with the oil in a large saucepan. Add the onion, garlic, celery and bacon and cook over a low heat, stirring occasionally, for 5 minutes, until softened. Stir in the tomatoes, tomato purée, sugar to taste and water and season to taste with salt and pepper. Increase the heat to medium and bring to the boil, then reduce the heat and simmer, stirring occasionally, for 15–20 minutes, until thickened.

2 Meanwhile, melt the butter with the oil in a large frying pan. Add the chicken and cook over a medium–high heat for 4–5 minutes on each side, until evenly browned.

3 Stir the basil and parsley into the sauce. Add the chicken and spoon the sauce over it. Cover and simmer for 10–15 minutes, until cooked through and tender. Garnish with parsley and serve immediately.

mexican drumsticks

serves 4
- 2 tbsp oil
- 8 chicken drumsticks
- 1 onion, finely chopped
- 1 tsp chilli powder
- 1 tsp ground coriander
- 400 g / 14 oz canned chopped tomatoes
- 2 tbsp tomato purée
- 125 g / 4½ oz frozen sweetcorn
- salt and pepper
- mixed pepper salad, to serve

1 Heat the oil in a large, heavy-based frying pan, add the chicken drumsticks and cook over a medium heat until lightly browned. Remove from the pan with a slotted spoon and set aside until required.

2 Add the onion to the pan and cook for 3–4 minutes, until softened, then stir in the chilli powder and coriander and cook for a few seconds, stirring briskly so the spices do not burn. Add the tomatoes and the tomato purée and stir well to combine.

3 Return the chicken drumsticks to the pan and simmer gently for 20 minutes, until the chicken is tender and thoroughly cooked. Add the sweetcorn and cook for a further 3–4 minutes. Season to taste with salt and pepper.

4 Serve hot with a mixed pepper salad.

cannelloni with chicken & ham

serves 4

- 1 tbsp olive oil, plus extra for brushing
- 1 small onion, finely chopped
- 175 g/6 oz fresh chicken mince
- 115 g/4 oz ham, finely chopped
- 70 g/2½ oz cream cheese with garlic and herbs
- 8 dried no-precook cannelloni tubes
- 4 tbsp grated Parmesan cheese
- salt and pepper

tomato sauce

- 25 g/1 oz butter
- 2 tbsp olive oil
- 1 onion, finely chopped
- 2 garlic cloves, finely chopped
- 1 celery stick, finely chopped
- 400 g/14 oz canned chopped tomatoes
- 2 tbsp tomato purée
- brown sugar, to taste
- 1 tbsp chopped fresh flat-leaf parsley
- 100 ml/3½ fl oz water
- salt and pepper

1 First, make the sauce. Melt the butter with the oil in a saucepan. Add the onion, garlic and celery and cook over a low heat, stirring occasionally, for 5 minutes, until softened. Stir in the tomatoes, tomato purée, sugar to taste, parsley and water and season to taste with salt and pepper. Increase the heat to medium and bring to the boil, then reduce the heat and simmer, stirring occasionally, for 20–30 minutes, until thickened.

2 Preheat the oven to 190°C/375°F/Gas Mark 5. Brush an ovenproof dish with oil. Heat the oil in a frying pan, add the onion and cook over a low heat, stirring occasionally, for 5 minutes, until softened. Add the chicken and cook, stirring frequently, for a further few minutes, until lightly browned. Remove the pan from the heat, stir in the ham and cream cheese and season to taste with salt and pepper.

3 Fill the cannelloni tubes with the chicken mixture and put them into the prepared dish. Pour the sauce over them, sprinkle with the Parmesan and bake in the preheated oven for 35–40 minutes. Serve immediately.

penne with chicken & feta

serves 4

- 2 tbsp olive oil
- 450 g/1 lb skinless, boneless chicken breasts, cut into thin strips
- 6 spring onions, chopped
- 225 g/8 oz feta cheese, diced
- 4 tbsp snipped fresh chives
- 450 g/1 lb dried penne
- salt and pepper

1 Heat the oil in a heavy-based frying pan. Add the chicken and cook over a medium heat, stirring frequently, for 5–8 minutes, or until golden all over and cooked through. Add the spring onions and cook for 2 minutes. Stir the feta cheese into the frying pan with half the chives and season to taste with salt and pepper.

2 Meanwhile, bring a large heavy-based saucepan of lightly salted water to the boil. Add the pasta, return to the boil and cook for 8–10 minutes, or until tender but still firm to the bite. Drain well, then transfer to a warmed serving dish.

3 Spoon the chicken mixture onto the pasta, toss lightly and serve immediately, garnished with the remaining chives.

chicken & mushroom tagliatelle

serves 4

- 25 g/1 oz dried shiitake mushrooms
- 350 ml/12 fl oz hot water
- 1 tbsp olive oil
- 6 bacon rashers, chopped
- 3 skinless, boneless chicken breasts, cut into strips
- 115 g/4 oz fresh shiitake mushrooms, sliced
- 1 small onion, finely chopped
- 1 tsp finely chopped fresh oregano or marjoram
- 250 ml/9 fl oz chicken stock
- 300 ml/10 fl oz whipping cream
- 450 g/1 lb dried tagliatelle
- 55 g/2 oz freshly grated Parmesan cheese
- salt and pepper
- chopped fresh flat-leaf parsley, to garnish

1 Put the dried mushrooms in a bowl with the hot water. Leave to soak for 30 minutes until softened. Remove, squeezing excess water back into the bowl. Strain the liquid through a fine-meshed sieve and reserve. Slice the soaked mushrooms, discarding the stems.

2 Heat the oil in a large frying pan over a medium heat. Add the bacon and chicken, then cook for about 3 minutes. Add the dried and fresh mushrooms, the onion and oregano. Cook for 5–7 minutes, until soft. Pour in the stock and the mushroom liquid. Bring to the boil, stirring. Simmer briskly for about 10 minutes, continuing to stir, until reduced. Add the cream and simmer for 5 minutes, stirring, until beginning to thicken. Season to taste with salt and pepper. Remove the pan from the heat and set aside.

3 Meanwhile, bring a large saucepan of lightly salted water to the boil. Add the pasta, bring back to the boil and cook for 8–10 minutes, or until tender but still firm to the bite. Drain and transfer to a serving dish. Pour the sauce over the pasta. Add half the Parmesan cheese and mix. Sprinkle with parsley and

fettuccine with chicken & onion cream sauce

serves 4

- 1 tbsp olive oil
- 2 tbsp butter
- 1 garlic clove, very finely chopped
- 4 skinless, boneless chicken breasts
- 1 onion, finely chopped
- 1 chicken stock cube, crumbled
- 125 ml/4 fl oz water
- 300 ml/10 fl oz double cream
- 175 ml/6 fl oz milk
- 6 spring onions, green part included, sliced diagonally
- 35 g/1¼ oz freshly grated Parmesan cheese
- 450 g/1 lb dried fettuccine
- salt and pepper
- chopped fresh flat-leaf parsley, to garnish

1 Heat the oil and butter with the garlic in a large frying pan over a medium–low heat. Cook the garlic until just beginning to colour. Add the chicken and increase the heat to medium. Cook for 4–5 minutes on each side, until the juices are no longer pink. Season to taste with salt and pepper. Remove from the heat. Remove the chicken from the pan, leaving the oil in the pan. Slice the chicken diagonally into thin strips and set aside.

2 Reheat the oil in the pan. Add the onion and gently cook for 5 minutes until soft. Add the crumbled stock cube and the water. Bring to the boil, then simmer over a medium–low heat for 10 minutes. Stir in the cream, milk, spring onions and Parmesan cheese. Simmer until heated through and slightly thickened.

3 Meanwhile, bring a large saucepan of lightly salted water to the boil. Add the pasta, bring back to the boil and cook for 8–10 minutes, or until tender but still firm to the bite. Drain and transfer to a warmed serving dish. Layer the chicken slices over the pasta. Pour over the sauce, garnish with parsley and serve.

penne with chicken & rocket

serves 4

- 25 g/1 oz butter
- 2 carrots, cut into thin batons
- 1 small onion, finely chopped
- 225 g/8 oz skinless, boneless chicken breasts, diced
- 225 g/8 oz mushrooms, quartered
- 125 ml/4 fl oz dry white wine
- 125 ml/4 fl oz chicken stock
- 2 garlic cloves, finely chopped
- 2 tbsp cornflour
- 4 tbsp water
- 2 tbsp single cream
- 125 ml/4 fl oz natural yogurt
- 2 tsp fresh thyme leaves, plus extra sprigs to garnish
- 115 g/4 oz rocket
- 350 g/12 oz dried penne
- salt and pepper

1 Melt the butter in a heavy-based frying pan. Add the carrots and cook over a medium heat, stirring frequently, for 2 minutes. Add the onion, chicken, mushrooms, wine, stock and garlic and season to taste with salt and pepper. Mix together the cornflour and water in a bowl until a smooth paste forms, then stir in the cream and yogurt. Stir the cornflour mixture into the frying pan with the thyme, cover and leave to simmer for 5 minutes. Place the rocket on top of the chicken, but do not stir in, cover and cook for 5 minutes, or until the chicken is tender.

2 Strain the cooking liquid into a saucepan, then transfer the chicken and vegetables to a dish and keep warm. Heat the cooking liquid, whisking occasionally, for 10 minutes, or until reduced and thickened.

3 Meanwhile, bring a large heavy-based saucepan of lightly salted water to the boil. Add the pasta, return to the boil and cook for 8–10 minutes, or until tender but still firm to the bite. Return the chicken and vegetables to the thickened cooking liquid and stir to coat.

4 Drain the pasta well, transfer to a warmed serving dish and spoon the chicken and vegetable mixture on top. Garnish with thyme sprigs and serve immediately.

spaghetti with parsley chicken

serves 4

- 1 tbsp olive oil
- thinly pared rind of 1 lemon, cut into julienne strips
- 1 tsp finely chopped fresh ginger
- 1 tsp sugar
- 225 ml/8 fl oz chicken stock
- 250 g/9 oz dried spaghetti
- 55 g/2 oz butter
- 225 g/8 oz skinless, boneless chicken breasts, diced
- 1 red onion, finely chopped
- leaves from 2 bunches of flat-leaf parsley
- salt

1 Heat the oil in a heavy-based saucepan. Add the lemon rind and cook over a low heat, stirring frequently, for 5 minutes. Stir in the ginger and sugar, season to taste with salt and cook, stirring constantly, for a further 2 minutes. Pour in the stock, bring to the boil, then cook for 5 minutes, or until the liquid has reduced by half.

2 Meanwhile, bring a large heavy-based saucepan of lightly salted water to the boil. Add the pasta, return to the boil and cook for 8–10 minutes, or until tender but still firm to the bite.

3 Melt half the butter in a frying pan. Add the chicken and onion and cook, stirring frequently, for 5 minutes, or until the chicken is lightly browned all over. Stir in the lemon and ginger mixture and cook for 1 minute. Stir in the parsley leaves and cook, stirring constantly, for a further 3 minutes.

4 Drain the pasta and transfer to a warmed serving dish, then add the remaining butter and toss well. Add the chicken sauce, toss again and serve.

fried chilli chicken

serves 4

- 750 g/1 lb 10 oz chicken thighs
- 3 tbsp lemon juice
- 1 tsp salt, or to taste
- 5 large garlic cloves, roughly chopped
- 5-cm/2-inch piece fresh ginger, roughly chopped
- 1 onion, roughly chopped
- 2 fresh red chillies, roughly chopped
- 4 tbsp groundnut oil
- 1 tsp ground turmeric
- ½ tsp chilli powder
- 150 ml/5 fl oz warm water
- 3–4 fresh green chillies
- cooked basmati rice, to serve

1 Put the chicken in a non-metallic bowl and rub in the lemon juice and salt. Set aside for 30 minutes.

2 Meanwhile, purée the garlic, ginger, onion and red chillies in a food processor or blender. Add a little water, if necessary, to help blade movement in a blender.

3 Heat the oil in a wide shallow pan, preferably non-stick, over a medium–high heat. When the oil is hot, cook the chicken in two batches, until golden brown on all sides. Drain on kitchen paper.

4 Add the fresh spice paste to the pan with the turmeric and chilli powder and reduce the heat to medium. Cook for 5–6 minutes, stirring regularly.

5 Add the chicken and warm water. Bring to the boil, reduce the heat to low, cover and cook for 20 minutes. Increase the heat to medium, cover and cook for a further 8–10 minutes, stirring halfway through to ensure that the thickened sauce does not stick to the base of the pan.

6 Remove the lid and cook until the sauce is reduced to a paste-like consistency, stirring regularly to prevent the sauce from sticking. Add the green chillies, cook for 2–3 minutes, remove from the heat and serve with basmati rice.

crispy-coated chicken breasts with wedges

serves 4
sweet potato wedges
- 4 large sweet potatoes, peeled and cut into wedges
- 4 tbsp vegetable oil
- 1 tsp chilli powder

crispy-coated chicken
- 50 g/1¾ oz hazelnuts, toasted and ground
- 25 g/1 oz dried white or wholemeal breadcrumbs
- 2 tbsp freshly grated pecorino cheese
- 1 tbsp chopped fresh parsley
- 4 skinless, boneless chicken breasts
- 1 egg, beaten
- 4 tbsp vegetable oil
- salt and pepper
- sprigs of fresh parsley, to garnish
- lemon wedges, to serve

1 Preheat the oven to 200°C/400°F/Gas Mark 6. To make the potato wedges, bring a large saucepan of water to the boil. Add the potatoes, cook over a medium heat for 5 minutes, then drain. Pour 2 tablespoons of the oil into a bowl and stir in the chilli powder. Add the potatoes and turn in the mixture until coated. Transfer to a baking sheet, drizzle over the remaining oil and bake for 35–40 minutes, turning frequently, until golden and cooked through.

2 About 15 minutes before the end of the cooking time, put the hazelnuts, breadcrumbs, cheese and parsley into a bowl, season to taste with salt and pepper and mix. Dip the chicken breasts into the egg, then coat in the breadcrumb mixture.

3 Heat the oil in a frying pan. Add the chicken and cook over a medium heat for 3–4 minutes on each side until golden. Lift out and drain on kitchen paper.

4 Remove the potatoes from the oven, divide between 4 serving plates and add a chicken breast to each. Garnish with parsley and serve with lemon wedges.

thai green chicken curry

serves 4

- 2 tbsp groundnut or sunflower oil
- 2 tbsp ready-made Thai green curry paste
- 500 g/1 lb 2 oz skinless boneless chicken breasts, cut into cubes
- 2 kaffir lime leaves, roughly torn
- 1 lemon grass stalk, finely chopped
- 225 ml/8 fl oz canned coconut milk
- 16 baby aubergines, halved
- 2 tbsp Thai fish sauce
- fresh Thai basil sprigs and kaffir lime leaves, thinly sliced, to garnish

1 Heat 2 tablespoons of oil in a preheated wok or large, heavy-based frying pan. Add 2 tablespoons of the curry paste and stir-fry briefly until all the aromas are released.

2 Add the chicken, lime leaves and lemon grass and stir-fry for 3–4 minutes, until the meat is beginning to colour. Add the coconut milk and aubergines and simmer gently for 8–10 minutes, or until tender.

3 Stir in the fish sauce and serve immediately, garnished with Thai basil sprigs and lime leaves.

easy chicken curry

serves 4

- 25 g/1 oz butter
- 4 tbsp olive oil
- 1 onion, finely chopped
- 2 garlic cloves, finely chopped
- 1 tbsp chopped fresh ginger
- 1 fresh green chilli, deseeded and chopped
- 1 celery stick, finely chopped
- 400 g/14 oz canned chopped tomatoes
- 2 tbsp tomato purée
- brown sugar, to taste
- ½ tsp ground cumin
- ½ tsp ground coriander
- ½ tsp ground turmeric
- ¼ tsp garam masala
- 100 ml/3½ fl oz water
- 600 g/1 lb 5 oz diced chicken
- 150 ml/5 fl oz double cream
- 200 g/7 oz baby spinach
- salt and pepper
- warm naan bread, to serve

1 Melt the butter with half the oil in a saucepan. Add the onion, garlic, ginger, chilli and celery and cook over a low heat, stirring occasionally, for 5 minutes, until softened. Stir in the tomatoes, tomato purée, sugar to taste, spices and water and season to taste with salt and pepper. Increase the heat to medium and bring to the boil, then reduce the heat and simmer, stirring occasionally, for 15–20 minutes, until thickened.

2 Meanwhile, heat the remaining oil in a frying pan. Add the chicken and cook over a medium heat, stirring frequently, for 5–7 minutes, until lightly browned all over. Remove with a slotted spoon.

3 Stir the chicken and cream into the sauce and simmer for 6 minutes, until the meat is tender and cooked through. Add the spinach and cook, stirring constantly, for 2–4 minutes, until wilted. Bring back to the boil, then transfer to a warmed serving dish. Serve immediately with naan bread.

chicken tikka masala

serves 4–6

- 30 g/1 oz ghee or 2 tbsp vegetable or groundnut oil
- 1 large garlic clove, finely chopped
- 1 fresh red chilli, deseeded and chopped
- 2 tsp ground cumin
- 2 tsp paprika
- 400 g/14 oz canned chopped tomatoes
- 300 ml/10 fl oz double cream
- 8 pieces cooked tandoori chicken
- salt and pepper
- sprigs of fresh coriander, to garnish

1 To make the tikka masala, heat the ghee in a large frying pan with a lid over a medium heat. Add the garlic and chilli and stir-fry for 1 minute. Stir in the cumin, paprika, and salt and pepper to taste and continue stirring for about 30 seconds.

2 Stir the tomatoes with their juices and the cream into the pan. Reduce the heat to low and leave the sauce to simmer for about 10 minutes, stirring frequently, until it reduces and thickens.

3 Meanwhile, remove all the bones and any skin from the tandoori chicken pieces, then cut the meat into bite-sized pieces.

4 Adjust the seasoning of the sauce, if necessary. Add the chicken pieces to the pan, cover and leave to simmer for 3–5 minutes until the chicken is heated through. Sprinkle with the coriander to serve.

chicken korma

serves 4

- 1 chicken, weighing 1.3 kg/3 lb
- 225 g/8 oz ghee or butter
- 3 onions, thinly sliced
- 1 garlic clove, crushed
- 2.5-cm/1-inch piece fresh root ginger, grated
- 1 tsp mild chilli powder
- 1 tsp ground turmeric
- 1 tsp ground coriander
- ½ tsp ground cardamom
- ½ tsp ground cinnamon
- ½ tsp salt
- 1 tbsp gram flour
- 125 ml/4 fl oz milk
- 500 ml/18 fl oz double cream
- fresh coriander leaves, to garnish
- freshly cooked rice, to serve

1 Put the chicken into a large saucepan, cover with water and bring to the boil. Reduce the heat, cover and simmer for 30 minutes. Remove from the heat, lift out the chicken and set aside to cool. Reserve 125 ml/4 fl oz of the cooking liquid. Remove and discard the skin and bones. Cut the flesh into bite-sized pieces.

2 Heat the ghee in a large saucepan over a medium heat. Add the onions and garlic and cook, stirring, for 3 minutes, or until softened. Add the ginger, chilli powder, turmeric, ground coriander, cardamom, cinnamon and salt and cook for a further 5 minutes. Add the chicken and the reserved cooking liquid. Cook for 2 minutes.

3 Blend the flour with a little of the milk and add to the pan, then stir in the remaining milk. Bring to the boil, stirring, then reduce the heat, cover and simmer for 25 minutes. Stir in the cream, cover and simmer for a further 15 minutes.

4 Garnish with coriander leaves and serve with freshly cooked rice.

Mmmm...
entertaining

roast chicken with cumin butter

serves 4

- 100 g/3½ oz butter, softened
- ½ tbsp cumin seeds, lightly crushed
- ½ preserved lemon, finely chopped
- 1 large garlic clove, crushed
- 1 whole chicken, about 1.5 kg/3 lb 5 oz
- salt and pepper
- roasted vegetables, to serve

1 Preheat the oven to 220°C/425°F/Gas Mark 7. Mash together the butter, cumin seeds, preserved lemon and garlic, and season to taste with salt and pepper. Using your fingers, loosen the skin on the chicken breasts and legs. Push most of the flavoured butter under the skin, moulding it to the shape of the bird. Smear any remaining butter over the skin.

2 Place the chicken in a roasting tin and cook in the preheated oven for 20 minutes. Reduce the temperature to 180°C/350°F/Gas Mark 4 and cook for a further 50–55 minutes, until the juices run clear when you pierce the thickest part of the chicken with a skewer. Transfer the chicken to a warmed serving dish, cover loosely with foil and leave to rest for 15 minutes.

3 Pour off most of the fat from the roasting tin. Place the tin over a medium heat and cook the juices for a few minutes, scraping any sediment from the base of the tin, until reduced slightly. Carve the chicken into slices, pour over the juices and serve with roasted vegetables.

italian chicken

serves 6

- 1 whole chicken, about 2.5 kg/5 lb 8 oz
- fresh rosemary sprigs
- 175 g/6 oz feta cheese, coarsely grated
- 2 tbsp sun-dried tomato purée
- 60 g/2 oz butter, softened
- 1 bulb garlic
- 1 kg/2 lb 4 oz new potatoes, halved if large
- 1 each red, green and yellow pepper, deseeded and cut into chunks
- 3 courgettes, thinly sliced
- 2 tbsp olive oil
- 2 tbsp plain flour
- 600 ml/1 pint chicken stock
- salt and pepper

1 Preheat the oven to 190°C/375°F/Gas Mark 5. Carefully cut between the skin and the top of the breast meat using a small pointed knife. Slide a finger into the slit and carefully enlarge it to form a pocket. Continue until the skin is completely lifted away from both breasts and the tops of the legs.

2 Chop the leaves from 3 rosemary stems. Mix with the feta cheese, sun-dried tomato purée, butter, and pepper to taste, then spoon under the skin. Put the chicken in a large roasting tin, cover with foil and cook in the preheated oven, calculating the cooking time as 20 minutes per 500 g/1 lb 2 oz, plus 20 minutes.

3 Break the garlic bulb into cloves but do not peel. Add the vegetables and garlic to the tin. After 40 minutes, drizzle with oil, tuck in some rosemary and season. Cook for the remaining calculated time, removing the foil for the last 40 minutes to brown the chicken.

4 Transfer the chicken and vegetables to a serving platter. Spoon the fat out of the roasting tin (it will be floating on top) and stir the flour into the remaining cooking juices. Place the roasting tin on top of the hob and cook over a medium heat for 2 minutes, then gradually stir in the stock. Bring to the boil, stirring until thickened and season to taste. Strain into a gravy boat and serve with the chicken.

coq au vin

serves 4
- 55 g/2 oz butter
- 2 tbsp olive oil
- 1.8 kg/4 lb chicken pieces
- 115 g/4 oz rindless smoked bacon, cut into strips
- 115 g/4 oz baby onions
- 115 g/4 oz chestnut mushrooms, halved
- 2 garlic cloves, finely chopped
- 2 tbsp brandy
- 225 ml/8 fl oz red wine
- 300 ml/10 fl oz chicken stock
- 1 bouquet garni
- 2 tbsp plain flour
- salt and pepper
- bay leaves, to garnish

1 Melt half the butter with the olive oil in a large, flameproof casserole. Add the chicken and cook over a medium heat, stirring, for 8–10 minutes, or until golden brown all over. Add the bacon, onions, mushrooms and garlic.

2 Pour in the brandy and set it alight with a match or taper. When the flames have died down, add the wine, stock and bouquet garni and season to taste with salt and pepper. Bring to the boil, reduce the heat and simmer gently for 1 hour, or until the chicken pieces are cooked through and tender. Meanwhile, make a beurre manié by mashing the remaining butter with the flour in a small bowl.

3 Remove and discard the bouquet garni. Transfer the chicken to a large plate and keep warm. Stir the beurre manié into the casserole, a little at a time. Bring to the boil, return the chicken to the casserole and serve immediately, garnished with bay leaves.

chicken pepperonata

serves 4

- 8 skinless chicken thighs
- 2 tbsp wholemeal flour
- 2 tbsp olive oil
- 1 small onion, thinly sliced
- 1 garlic clove, crushed
- 1 each large red, yellow and green peppers, deseeded and thinly sliced
- 400 g/14 oz canned chopped tomatoes
- 1 tbsp chopped fresh oregano, plus extra to garnish
- salt and pepper
- crusty wholemeal bread, to serve

1 Toss the chicken thighs in the flour, shaking off the excess.

2 Heat the oil in a wide frying pan and cook the chicken quickly until sealed and lightly browned, then remove from the pan.

3 Add the onion to the pan and cook gently until soft. Add the garlic, peppers, tomatoes and oregano, then bring to the boil, stirring.

4 Arrange the chicken over the vegetables, season well with salt and pepper, then cover the pan tightly and simmer for 20–25 minutes or until the chicken is completely cooked and tender.

5 Taste and adjust the seasoning, if necessary. Garnish with oregano and serve with crusty wholemeal bread.

chicken in white wine

serves 4

- 55 g/2 oz butter
- 2 tbsp olive oil
- 2 rindless, thick streaky bacon rashers, chopped
- 115 g/4 oz baby onions, peeled
- 1 garlic clove, finely chopped
- 1.8 kg/4 lb chicken pieces
- 400 ml/14 fl oz dry white wine
- 300 ml/10 fl oz chicken stock
- 1 bouquet garni
- 115 g/4 oz button mushrooms
- 25 g/1 oz plain flour
- salt and pepper
- fresh mixed herbs, to garnish

1 Preheat the oven to 160°C/325°F/Gas Mark 3. Melt half the butter with the oil in a flameproof casserole. Add the bacon and cook over a medium heat, stirring, for 5–10 minutes, or until golden brown. Transfer the bacon to a large plate. Add the onions and garlic to the casserole and cook over a low heat, stirring occasionally, for 10 minutes, or until golden. Transfer to the plate. Add the chicken and cook over a medium heat, stirring constantly, for 8–10 minutes, or until golden. Transfer to the plate.

2 Drain off any excess fat from the casserole. Stir in the wine and stock and bring to the boil, scraping any sediment off the base. Add the bouquet garni and season to taste. Return the bacon, onions and chicken to the casserole. Cover and cook in the preheated oven for 1 hour. Add the mushrooms, re-cover and cook for 15 minutes. Meanwhile, make a beurre manié by mashing the remaining butter with the flour in a small bowl.

3 Remove the casserole from the oven and set over a medium heat. Remove and discard the bouquet garni. Whisk in the beurre manié, a little at a time. Bring to the boil, stirring constantly, then serve, garnished with fresh herbs.

spiced chicken stew

serves 6

- 1.8 kg/4 lb chicken pieces
- 2 tbsp paprika
- 2 tbsp olive oil
- 25 g/1 oz butter
- 450 g/1 lb onions, chopped
- 2 yellow peppers, deseeded and chopped
- 400 g/14 oz canned chopped tomatoes
- 225 ml/8 fl oz dry white wine
- 450 ml/16 fl oz chicken stock
- 1 tbsp Worcestershire sauce
- ½ tsp Tabasco
- 1 tbsp finely chopped fresh parsley
- 325 g/11½ oz canned sweetcorn kernels, drained
- 425 g/15 oz canned butter beans, drained and rinsed
- 2 tbsp plain flour
- 4 tbsp water
- salt
- fresh parsley sprigs, to garnish

1 Season the chicken pieces with salt and dust with paprika.

2 Heat the oil and butter in a flameproof casserole or large saucepan. Add the chicken pieces and cook over a medium heat, turning, for 10–15 minutes, or until golden. Transfer to a plate with a slotted spoon.

3 Add the onions and peppers to the casserole. Cook over a low heat, stirring occasionally, for 5 minutes, or until softened. Add the tomatoes, wine, stock, Worcestershire sauce, Tabasco sauce and parsley and bring to the boil, stirring. Return the chicken to the casserole, cover and simmer, stirring occasionally, for 30 minutes.

4 Add the sweetcorn and beans to the casserole, partially re-cover and simmer for a further 30 minutes. Place the flour and water in a small bowl and mix to make a paste. Stir a ladleful of the cooking liquid into the paste, then stir it into the stew. Cook, stirring frequently, for 5 minutes. Serve, garnished with parsley.

hunter's chicken

serves 4

- 15 g/½ oz unsalted butter
- 2 tbsp olive oil
- 1.8 kg/4 lb skinned chicken pieces
- 2 red onions, sliced
- 2 garlic cloves, finely chopped
- 400 g/14 oz canned chopped tomatoes
- 2 tbsp chopped fresh flat-leaf parsley
- 6 fresh basil leaves, torn
- 1 tbsp sun-dried tomato purée
- 150 ml/5 fl oz red wine
- 225 g/8 oz mushrooms, sliced
- salt and pepper

1 Preheat the oven to 160°C/325°F/Gas Mark 3. Heat the butter and oil in a flameproof casserole and cook the chicken over a medium–high heat, turning frequently, for 10 minutes, or until golden all over and sealed. Using a slotted spoon, transfer to a plate.

2 Add the onions and garlic to the casserole and cook over a low heat, stirring occasionally, for 10 minutes, or until softened and golden. Add the tomatoes with their juice, the herbs, sun-dried tomato purée and wine, and season to taste with salt and pepper. Bring to the boil, then return the chicken portions to the casserole, pushing them down into the sauce.

3 Cover and cook in the preheated oven for 50 minutes. Add the mushrooms and cook for a further 10 minutes, or until the chicken is tender and the juices run clear when a skewer is inserted into the thickest part of the meat. Serve immediately.

sunshine chicken

serves 4

- 450 g/1 lb skinless, boneless chicken
- 1½ tbsp plain flour
- 1 tbsp olive oil
- 1 onion, cut into wedges
- 2 celery sticks, sliced
- 150 ml/5 fl oz orange juice
- 300 ml/10 fl oz chicken stock
- 1 tbsp light soy sauce
- 1–2 tsp clear honey
- 1 tbsp grated orange rind
- 1 orange pepper, deseeded and chopped
- 225 g/8 oz courgettes, sliced into half moons
- 2 small corn on the cob, halved, or 100 g/3½ oz baby sweetcorn
- 1 orange, peeled and segmented
- salt and pepper
- 1 tbsp chopped fresh parsley, to garnish

1 Lightly rinse the chicken and pat dry with kitchen paper. Cut into bite-sized pieces. Season the flour well with salt and pepper. Toss the chicken in the seasoned flour until well coated and reserve any remaining seasoned flour.

2 Heat the oil in a large, heavy-based frying pan and cook the chicken over a high heat, stirring frequently, for 5 minutes, or until golden on all sides and sealed. Using a slotted spoon, transfer the chicken to a plate.

3 Add the onion and celery to the frying pan and cook over a medium heat, stirring frequently, for 5 minutes, or until softened. Sprinkle in the reserved seasoned flour and cook, stirring constantly, for 2 minutes, then remove from the heat. Gradually stir in the orange juice, stock, soy sauce and honey, followed by the orange rind, then return to the heat and bring to the boil, stirring.

4 Return the chicken to the frying pan. Reduce the heat, cover and simmer, stirring occasionally, for 15 minutes. Add the orange pepper, courgettes and corn on the cob and simmer for a further 10 minutes, or until the chicken and vegetables are tender. Add the orange segments, stir well and heat through for 1 minute. Serve garnished with the parsley.

chicken with garlic

serves 6

- 4 tbsp plain flour
- Spanish paprika, either hot or smoked sweet, to taste
- 1 large chicken, about 1.75 kg/3 lb 12 oz, cut into 8 pieces, rinsed and patted dry
- 4–6 tbsp olive oil
- 24 large garlic cloves, peeled and halved
- 450 ml/¾ pint chicken stock
- 4 tbsp dry white wine, such as white Rioja
- 2 sprigs of fresh flat-leaf parsley, 1 bay leaf and 1 sprig of fresh thyme, tied together
- salt and pepper
- fresh flat-leaf parsley and thyme leaves, to garnish

1 Sift the flour onto a large plate and season with paprika and salt and pepper to taste. Coat the chicken pieces with the flour on both sides, shaking off the excess. Heat 4 tablespoons of the oil in a large, deep frying pan or flameproof casserole over a medium heat. Add the garlic and fry, stirring frequently, for about 2 minutes to flavour the oil. Remove the garlic with a slotted spoon and set aside to drain on kitchen paper.

2 Working in batches, add the chicken pieces to the pan, skin-side down, adding a little extra oil if necessary. Fry for 5 minutes until the skin is golden brown. Turn over and fry for 5 minutes more, then transfer to a plate.

3 Pour off any excess oil. Return the garlic and chicken pieces to the pan and add the stock, wine and herbs. Bring to the boil, then reduce the heat, cover and simmer for 20–25 minutes until the chicken is cooked through and tender and the garlic is very soft.

4 Transfer the chicken pieces to a serving platter and keep warm. Bring the cooking liquid to the boil, with the garlic and herbs, and boil until reduced to about 300 ml/½ pint. Remove and discard the cooked herbs. Taste and adjust the seasoning, if necessary. Spoon the sauce and the garlic cloves over the chicken pieces. Garnish with fresh parsley and thyme.

louisiana chicken

serves 4
- 5 tbsp sunflower oil
- 4 chicken pieces
- 55 g/2 oz plain flour
- 1 onion, chopped
- 2 celery sticks, sliced
- 1 green pepper, deseeded and chopped
- 2 garlic cloves, finely chopped
- 2 tsp chopped fresh thyme
- 2 fresh red chillies, deseeded and finely chopped
- 400 g/14 oz canned chopped tomatoes
- 300 ml/10 fl oz chicken stock
- salt and pepper
- lamb's lettuce and chopped fresh thyme, to garnish

1 Heat the oil in a large, heavy-based saucepan or flameproof casserole. Add the chicken and cook over a medium heat, stirring, for 5–10 minutes, or until golden. Transfer the chicken to a plate with a slotted spoon.

2 Stir the flour into the oil and cook over a very low heat, stirring constantly, for 15 minutes, or until light golden. Do not let it burn. Add the onion, celery and green pepper and cook, stirring constantly, for 2 minutes. Add the garlic, thyme and chillies and cook, stirring, for 1 minute.

3 Stir in the tomatoes and their juices, then gradually stir in the stock. Return the chicken pieces to the saucepan, cover and simmer for 45 minutes, or until the chicken is cooked through and tender. Season to taste with salt and pepper, transfer to warmed serving plates and serve immediately, garnished with some lettuce leaves and a sprinkling of chopped thyme.

chicken tagine

serves 4

- 1 tbsp olive oil
- 1 onion, cut into small wedges
- 2–4 garlic cloves, sliced
- 450 g/1 lb skinless, boneless chicken breast, diced
- 1 tsp ground cumin
- 2 cinnamon sticks, lightly bruised
- 1 tbsp plain wholemeal flour
- 225 g/8 oz aubergine, diced
- 1 red pepper, deseeded and chopped
- 85 g/3 oz button mushrooms, sliced
- 1 tbsp tomato purée
- 600 ml/1 pint chicken stock
- 280 g/10 oz canned chickpeas, drained and rinsed
- 55 g/2 oz ready-to-eat dried apricots, chopped
- salt and pepper
- 1 tbsp chopped fresh coriander, to garnish

1 Heat the oil in a large saucepan over a medium heat, add the onion and garlic and cook for 3 minutes, stirring frequently. Add the chicken and cook, stirring constantly, for a further 5 minutes, or until sealed on all sides. Add the cumin and cinnamon sticks to the saucepan halfway through sealing the chicken.

2 Sprinkle in the flour and cook, stirring constantly, for 2 minutes. Add the aubergine, red pepper and mushrooms and cook for a further 2 minutes, stirring constantly.

3 Blend the tomato purée with the stock, stir into the saucepan and bring to the boil. Reduce the heat and add the chickpeas and apricots. Cover and simmer for 15–20 minutes, or until the chicken is tender.

4 Season with salt and pepper to taste and serve immediately, sprinkled with coriander.

spanish chicken with tomato & chocolate sauce

serves 6
- 6 chicken pieces
- plain flour, for dusting
- 4 tbsp olive oil

tomato & chocolate sauce
- 25 g/1 oz butter
- 2 tbsp olive oil
- 1 onion, finely chopped
- 2 garlic cloves, finely chopped
- 1 red pepper, deseeded and sliced
- 800 g/1 lb 12 oz canned chopped tomatoes
- 2 tbsp tomato purée
- brown sugar, to taste
- ½ tsp ground nutmeg
- ½ tsp ground cinnamon
- ¼ tsp ground cloves
- 250 ml/9 fl oz dry white wine
- 70 g/2½ oz dark chocolate, finely chopped, plus extra grated chocolate to garnish
- salt and pepper

1 Dust the chicken portions with flour. Heat the oil in a large frying pan. Add the chicken, in batches if necessary, and cook over a medium heat, turning occasionally, for 8–10 minutes, until evenly browned. Remove the chicken from the pan and drain on kitchen paper.

2 Drain off the fat from the pan and wipe out with kitchen paper. To make the sauce, melt the butter with the oil in the same pan. Add the onion, garlic and red pepper and cook over a low heat, stirring occasionally, for 5 minutes, until softened. Stir in the tomatoes, tomato purée, sugar to taste, nutmeg, cinnamon, cloves and wine and season to taste with salt and pepper. Increase the heat to medium and bring to the boil.

3 Return the chicken to the pan, reduce the heat, cover and simmer for 20 minutes. Remove the lid from the pan and simmer for a further 20 minutes, until the chicken is cooked through and tender and the sauce has thickened. Add the chopped chocolate and stir constantly until it has melted. Garnish with grated chocolate and serve immediately.

chicken with tomato sauce & melted mozzarella

serves 6

- 6 rashers bacon
- 25 g/1 oz butter
- 2 tsp chopped fresh tarragon
- 6 skinless, boneless chicken breasts, about 175 g/6 oz each
- 115 g/4 oz mozzarella cheese, sliced

rich tomato sauce

- 25 g/1 oz butter
- 2 tbsp olive oil
- 1 onion, finely chopped
- 2 garlic cloves, finely chopped
- 1 celery stick, finely chopped
- 400 g/14 oz canned chopped tomatoes
- 2 tbsp tomato purée
- brown sugar, to taste
- 1 tsp dried oregano
- 100 ml/3½ fl oz water
- salt and pepper

1 First, make the sauce. Melt the butter with the oil in a saucepan. Add the onion, garlic and celery and cook over a low heat, stirring occasionally, for 5 minutes, until softened. Stir in the tomatoes, tomato purée, sugar to taste, oregano and water and season to taste with salt and pepper. Increase the heat to medium and bring to the boil, then reduce the heat and simmer, stirring occasionally, for 15–20 minutes, until thickened.

2 Meanwhile, fry the bacon without any additional fat in a large frying pan over a medium heat for 5 minutes. Remove with tongs and drain on kitchen paper. Add the butter to the pan and, when it has melted, stir in the tarragon, add the chicken and cook, turning occasionally, for 15–20 minutes, until cooked through and tender.

3 Preheat the grill. Transfer the chicken to an ovenproof dish and put a bacon rasher on top of each breast. Pour the sauce over them, cover with the mozzarella slices and cook under the preheated grill for 4–5 minutes, until the cheese has melted and is lightly browned. Serve immediately.

chicken in tomato & almond sauce

serves 4

- 25 g/1 oz butter
- 2 tbsp olive oil
- 2 shallots, finely chopped
- 3 garlic cloves, finely chopped
- 1 celery stick, finely chopped
- 55 g/2 oz ground almonds
- 4 tbsp fresh breadcrumbs
- 3 tbsp chopped fresh flat-leaf parsley, plus extra to garnish
- 500 g/1 lb 2 oz plum tomatoes, peeled, cored and chopped
- 2 tbsp tomato purée
- brown sugar, to taste
- 4 skinless, boneless chicken breasts
- 1 litre/1¾ pints hot chicken stock
- juice of ½ orange
- 1 bouquet garni
- 6 black peppercorns
- 2 tbsp flaked almonds
- salt and pepper

1 Melt the butter with the oil in a saucepan. Add the shallots, garlic and celery and cook over a low heat, stirring occasionally, for 5 minutes, until softened. Remove the pan from the heat and stir in the ground almonds, breadcrumbs, parsley, tomatoes, tomato purée and sugar to taste. Season to taste with salt and pepper. Return the pan to the heat and cook, stirring constantly, for 5 minutes, or until thickened. Remove the pan from the heat.

2 Put the chicken into a large, shallow pan. Pour in the hot stock and orange juice, add the bouquet garni and peppercorns and bring just to the boil. Reduce the heat so that the water is barely shivering, cover and poach for 20 minutes, until the chicken is cooked through and tender.

3 Transfer the chicken to a warmed serving dish and keep warm. Strain and reserve 5 tablespoons of the cooking liquid, then stir it into the sauce. Return the pan to the heat and cook, stirring constantly, until thoroughly combined and heated through. Pour the sauce over the chicken and sprinkle with the flaked almonds. Garnish with parsley and serve immediately.

paella

serves 6–8

- 16 live mussels, scrubbed and debearded
- ½ tsp saffron threads
- 2 tbsp hot water
- 350 g/12 oz paella rice
- 6 tbsp olive oil
- 6–8 unboned, skin-on chicken thighs, excess skin removed
- 140 g/5 oz chorizo, casing removed, cut into 5-mm/¼-inch slices
- 2 large onions, chopped
- 4 large garlic cloves, crushed
- 1 tsp paprika
- 100 g/3½ oz green beans, chopped
- 125 g/4½ oz frozen peas
- 1.3 litres/2¼ pints fish, chicken or vegetable stock
- 16 raw prawns, peeled and deveined
- 2 roasted red peppers, sliced
- 35 g/1¼ oz fresh chopped parsley, to garnish
- salt and pepper

1 Discard any mussels with broken shells and any that refuse to close when tapped. Soak in lightly salted water for 10 minutes. Put the saffron and water in a cup and leave to infuse for a few minutes. Meanwhile, put the rice in a sieve and rinse in cold water until the water runs clear.

2 Heat 3 tablespoons of the oil in a paella pan or ovenproof casserole. Cook the chicken over medium–high heat, turning frequently, for 5 minutes, or until golden. Transfer to a bowl. Add the chorizo to the pan and cook, stirring, for 1 minute, or until beginning to crisp. Add to the chicken. Heat the remaining oil in the pan and cook the onions, stirring frequently, for 2 minutes, then add the garlic and paprika and cook for a further 3 minutes, or until the onions are softened.

3 Add the drained rice, beans and peas and stir until coated in oil. Return the chicken and chorizo with any juices to the pan. Stir in the stock, saffron and its soaking liquid, and salt and pepper to taste and bring to the boil, stirring. Reduce the heat to low and simmer, uncovered and without stirring, for 15 minutes, or until the rice is almost tender and most of the liquid has been absorbed.

4 Arrange the mussels, prawns and red peppers on top, then cover and simmer, without stirring, for a further 5 minutes, or until the prawns turn pink and the mussels open. Discard any mussels that remain closed. Sprinkle with the parsley and serve immediately.

chicken risotto with saffron

serves 4

- 125 g/4½ oz butter
- 900 g/2 lb skinless, boneless chicken breasts, thinly sliced
- 1 large onion, chopped
- 500 g/1 lb 2 oz risotto rice
- 150 ml/5 fl oz white wine
- 1 tsp crumbled saffron threads
- 1.3 litres/2¼ pints hot chicken stock
- 55 g/2 oz Parmesan cheese, grated
- salt and pepper

1 Heat 55 g/2 oz of the butter in a deep saucepan. Add the chicken and onion and cook, stirring frequently, for 8 minutes, or until golden brown.

2 Add the rice and mix to coat in the butter. Cook, stirring constantly, for 2–3 minutes, or until the grains are translucent.

3 Add the wine and cook, stirring constantly, for 1 minute, until reduced.

4 Mix the saffron with 4 tablespoons of the hot stock. Add the liquid to the rice and cook, stirring constantly, until it is absorbed.

5 Gradually add the remaining hot stock, a ladleful at a time. Add more liquid as the rice absorbs each addition. Cook, stirring, for 20 minutes, or until all the liquid is absorbed and the rice is creamy.

6 Remove from the heat and add the remaining butter. Mix well, then stir in the Parmesan until it melts. Season to taste with salt and pepper. Spoon the risotto into warmed serving dishes and serve immediately.

baked tapenade chicken

serves 4

- 4 skinless, boneless chicken breasts
- 4 tbsp green olive tapenade
- 8 thin slices smoked pancetta
- 2 garlic cloves, chopped
- 250 g/9 oz cherry tomatoes, halved
- 100 ml/3½ fl oz dry white wine
- 2 tbsp olive oil
- 8 slices ciabatta
- salt and pepper

1 Preheat the oven to 220°C/425°F/Gas Mark 7. Place the chicken breasts on a board and cut three deep slashes into each.

2 Spread a tablespoon of the tapenade over each chicken breast, pushing it into the slashes with a palette knife. Wrap each chicken breast in two slices of pancetta. Place the chicken breasts in a shallow ovenproof dish and arrange the garlic and tomatoes around them. Season to taste with salt and pepper, then pour over the wine and 1 tablespoon of the oil.

3 Bake in the preheated oven for about 20 minutes, until the juices run clear when the chicken is pierced with a skewer. Cover the dish loosely with foil and leave to stand for 5 minutes.

4 Meanwhile, preheat the grill to high. Brush the ciabatta with the remaining oil and cook under the preheated grill for 2–3 minutes, turning once, until golden. Transfer the chicken and tomatoes to serving plates and spoon over the juices. Serve with the toasted ciabatta.

steamed chicken with chilli & coriander butter

serves 4
- 55 g/2 oz butter, softened
- 1 fresh bird's eye chilli, deseeded and chopped
- 3 tbsp chopped fresh coriander
- 4 skinless, boneless chicken breasts, about 175 g/6 oz each
- 400 ml/14 fl oz coconut milk
- 350 ml/12 fl oz chicken stock
- 200 g/7 oz basmati rice
- salt and pepper

pickled vegetables
- 1 carrot
- ½ cucumber
- 3 spring onions
- 2 tbsp rice vinegar

1 Mix the butter with the chilli and coriander. Cut a deep slash into the side of each chicken breast to form a pocket. Spoon a quarter of the butter into each pocket and place on a 30-cm/12-inch square of baking paper. Season to taste with salt and pepper, then bring two opposite sides of the paper together on top, folding over to seal firmly. Twist the ends to seal.

2 Pour the coconut milk and stock into a large pan with a steamer top. Bring to the boil. Stir in the rice with a pinch of salt. Place the chicken parcels in the steamer top, cover and simmer for 15–18 minutes, stirring the rice once, until the rice is tender and the chicken is cooked through.

3 Meanwhile, trim the carrot, cucumber and spring onions and cut into fine matchsticks. Sprinkle with the rice vinegar. Unwrap the chicken, reserving the juices, and cut in half diagonally. Serve the chicken over the rice, with the juices spooned over and the pickled vegetables on the side.

chicken, mushroom & cashew nut risotto

serves 4

- 55 g/2 oz butter
- 1 onion, chopped
- 250 g/9 oz skinless, boneless chicken breasts, diced
- 350 g/12 oz risotto rice
- 1 tsp ground turmeric
- 350 ml/12 fl oz white wine
- 1.3 litres/2¼ pints simmering chicken stock
- 75 g/2¾ oz chestnut mushrooms, sliced
- 50 g/1¾ oz cashew nuts, halved
- salt and pepper

to garnish

- wild rocket
- fresh Parmesan cheese shavings
- fresh basil leaves

1 Melt the butter in a large saucepan over a medium heat. Add the onion and cook, stirring occasionally, for 5 minutes, or until soft. Add the chicken and cook, stirring frequently, for a further 5 minutes. Reduce the heat, add the rice and mix to coat in butter. Cook, stirring constantly, for 2–3 minutes, or until the grains are translucent. Stir in the turmeric, then add the wine. Cook, stirring constantly, for 1 minute until reduced.

2 Gradually add the stock, a ladleful at a time. Stir constantly and add more liquid as the rice absorbs each addition. Increase the heat to medium so that the liquid bubbles. Cook for 20 minutes, or until all the liquid is absorbed and the rice is creamy. About 3 minutes before the end of the cooking time, stir in the mushrooms and cashew nuts. Season to taste with salt and pepper.

3 Remove the risotto from the heat and spoon into individual serving dishes. Sprinkle over the rocket, Parmesan cheese shavings and basil leaves and serve.

chilli chicken with chickpea mash

serves 4

- 4 skinless, boneless chicken breasts, about 140 g/5 oz each
- 1 tbsp olive oil
- 8 tsp harissa (chilli) paste
- salt and pepper

chickpea mash

- 2 tbsp olive oil
- 2–3 garlic cloves, crushed
- 400 g/14 oz canned chickpeas, drained and rinsed
- 4 tbsp milk
- 3 tbsp chopped fresh coriander, plus extra to garnish
- salt and pepper

1 Make shallow cuts in each chicken breast. Place the chicken in a dish, brush with the oil and coat both sides with the harissa paste. Season well with salt and pepper, cover the dish with foil and marinate in the refrigerator for 30 minutes.

2 Preheat the oven to 220°C/425°F/Gas Mark 7. Transfer the chicken breasts to a roasting tin and roast for about 20–30 minutes until they are cooked through and the juices run clear when a skewer is inserted into the thickest part of the meat.

3 Meanwhile, make the chickpea mash. Heat the oil in a saucepan and gently cook the garlic for 1 minute, then add the chickpeas and milk and heat through for a few minutes. Transfer to a blender or food processor and purée until smooth. Season to taste with salt and pepper and stir in the coriander.

4 To serve, slice the chicken breasts. Divide the chickpea mash between 4 serving plates, top each one with a sliced chicken breast and garnish with coriander.

roasted chicken with sun-blush tomato pesto

serves 4
- 4 skinless, boneless chicken breasts, about 800 g/1 lb 12 oz in total
- 1 tbsp olive oil
- mixed salad, to serve

red pesto
- 125 g/4½ oz sun-blush tomatoes in oil (drained weight), chopped
- 2 garlic cloves, crushed
- 6 tbsp pine kernels, lightly toasted
- 150 ml/5 fl oz extra virgin olive oil

1 Preheat the oven to 200°C/400°F/Gas Mark 6. To make the red pesto, put the sun-blush tomatoes, garlic, 4 tablespoons of the pine kernels and the extra virgin olive oil into a food processor and blend to a coarse paste.

2 Arrange the chicken in a large, ovenproof dish or roasting tin. Brush the chicken breasts with the olive oil, then place a tablespoon of the red pesto on top of each. Using the back of a spoon, spread the pesto so that it covers the top of the chicken. (Store any remaining pesto in an airtight container in the refrigerator for up to 1 week.)

3 Roast the chicken in the preheated oven for 30 minutes, or until tender and the juices run clear when a skewer is inserted into the thickest part of the meat.

4 Sprinkle with the remaining pine kernels and serve with a mixed salad.

buttered chicken parcels

serves 4

- 4 tbsp butter
- 4 shallots, finely chopped
- 300 g/10½ oz frozen spinach, defrosted
- 450 g/1 lb blue cheese, such as Stilton, crumbled
- 1 egg, lightly beaten
- 1 tbsp snipped fresh chives
- 1 tbsp chopped fresh oregano
- 4 skinless, boneless chicken breasts
- 8 slices Parma ham
- salt and pepper
- baby spinach leaves, to serve
- fresh chives, to garnish

1 Melt half of the butter in a frying pan over a medium heat. Add the shallots and cook, stirring, for 4 minutes. Remove from the heat and leave to cool for 10 minutes.

2 Preheat the oven to 180°C/350°F/Gas Mark 4. Using your hands, squeeze out as much moisture from the defrosted spinach as possible. Transfer the spinach into a large bowl, add the shallots, cheese, egg, herbs and salt and pepper to taste. Mix together well.

3 Halve each chicken breast then put each piece between 2 sheets of clingfilm and pound gently with a rolling pin to flatten to an even thickness. Spoon some cheese mixture into the centre of each piece, then roll it up. Wrap each roll in a slice of Parma ham and secure with a cocktail stick. Transfer to a roasting dish, dot with the remaining butter and bake in the preheated oven for 30 minutes until golden.

4 Divide the baby spinach leaves between 4 serving plates. Remove the chicken from the oven and place 2 chicken rolls on each plate. Garnish with fresh chives and serve.

chicken & spicy tomato sauce parcels

serves 4
- 4 chicken breasts, about 175 g/6 oz each
- 4 fresh tarragon sprigs

spicy tomato sauce
- 25 g/1 oz butter
- 2 tbsp olive oil
- 1 onion, finely chopped
- 2 garlic cloves, finely chopped
- 1 celery stick, finely chopped
- 2 orange peppers, deseeded and chopped
- 400 g/14 oz canned chopped tomatoes
- 2 tbsp sun-dried tomato paste
- brown sugar, to taste
- 1 tbsp paprika
- 1 tsp chilli powder
- 1 tsp dried thyme
- 100 ml/3½ fl oz water
- salt and pepper

1 First, make the sauce. Melt the butter with the oil in a saucepan. Add the onion, garlic, celery and peppers and cook over a low heat, stirring occasionally, for 5 minutes, until softened. Stir in the tomatoes, sun-dried tomato paste, sugar to taste, paprika, chilli powder, thyme and water and season to taste with salt and pepper. Increase the heat to medium and bring to the boil, then reduce the heat and simmer, stirring occasionally, for 15–20 minutes, until thickened.

2 Meanwhile, preheat the oven to 190°C/375°F/Gas Mark 5. Cut four squares of greaseproof paper, each large enough to enclose a chicken breast. Put one chicken breast on each square.

3 Divide the sauce among the chicken breasts and top each with a tarragon sprig. Fold the paper over fairly loosely and double-fold the edges to seal. Put the parcels on a baking sheet and bake in the preheated oven for 35–40 minutes, until the chicken is cooked through and tender. Serve immediately.

Index

223